C000181303

SPEEDWAY IN
EAST ANGLIA

SPEEDWAY IN EAST ANGLIA

Compiled by
Norman Jacobs

TEMPUS

First published 2000

Published by:
Tempus Publishing Limited
The Mill, Brimscombe Port
Stroud, Gloucestershire, GL5 2QG

© Norman Jacobs, 2000

The right of Norman Jacobs to be identified as the Author
of this work has been asserted by them in accordance with the
Copyrights, Designs and Patents Act 1988.

Typesetting and origination by Tempus Publishing Ltd.
Printed and bound in Great Britain

All rights reserved. No part of this book may be reprinted or reproduced or
utilised in any form or by any electronic, mechanical or other means, now known
or hereafter invented, including photocopying and recording, or in any
information storage or retrieval system, without the permission in writing from
the Publishers.

British Library Cataloguing in Publication Data.
A catalogue record for this book is available from the British Library

ISBN 07524 1882 3

Also available from Tempus Publishing

The Five Nations Story	D. Hands	0 7524 1851 3
The Football Programme	J. Litster	0 7524 1855 6
Forever England	M. Shaoul/T. Williamson	0 7524 2042 9
Leeds United in Europe	D. Saffer	0 7524 2043 7
Tottenham Hotspur: 1882-1952	R. Brazier	0 7524 2044 5

Contents

KING'S OAK SPEEDWAY, HIGH BEECH, LOUGHTON, ESSEX
(By kind permission of L. W. S. MARDEN, Esq.)

PROGRAMME of . .

DIRT TRACK RACING

Organised by the ILFORD MOTOR CYCLE & LIGHT CAR CLUB under A.C.U Permit. Restricted to the following Clubs :
Ilford M.C. & L.C.C. and Colchester Motor Club.

SUNDAY, FEBRUARY 19th, 1928, at 10.30 a.m.

Officials :

Eastern Centre Stewd.—M R.W. FISON, Esq.   Judges—E. J. BASS, Esq. (Essex M.C.), C. BAXTER, Esq. (Ilford), P. COX, Esq. (Ilford).
Timekeeper and Starter—RAY ARBOT, Esq. (Essex M.C.).

Lap Scorers—O. VERRALL, Esq. (Ilford), P. CLIFTON, Esq. (Colchester).   Finance—D. PAGE, Esq. (Ilford).
Marshals—Members of Clubs.   Marshal in Charge—A. BELLAMY, Esq. (Ilford).

Spectators must keep to the inner portion of the track behind ropes.

No dogs allowed inside under any consideration.

Spectators will only be allowed to cross track between events and at one place only.

If Competitors fall they must be left to the Marshals. On no account must the public invade the track.

These rules are laid down by the Governing Body, the Auto-Cycle Union and unless strictly adhered to the Stewards of the Meeting have power to stop this event and also further events.

Please help all you can.   Thank you !

ADMISSION SIXPENCE   PROGRAMME TWOPENCE
CAR PARK under supervision. Cars 6d., Cycles and Three-wheelers 3d.
LUNCHEONS : 4/- (Table d'Hote), 3/-   Hon. Organising Secretary :
TEAS, 1/6   R. J. HILL-BAILEY,
These must be booked from the Hotel if wanted.   41, Hickling Road, Ilford.

Opening announcement for Britain's first ever speedway meeting at High Beech on 19 February 1928.

Acknowledgements

This book would not have been possible without all the time and help so freely given by many speedway supporters in East Anglia and I should like to thank the following in particular for their help in various ways: Ken Taylor, Keith Farman, Mike Kemp, Bob Miller, Brian Tungate, Terry Ripo, Terry Catley, Paul 'Bart' Simpson, Graham Fraser, John Hannant and Mr J.E. Woodcock.

I would also like to acknowledge the debt I owe to all those writers and statisticians of the past and present who have made my task so much easier. In particular, Peter Oakes, whose unrivalled output on the subject of speedway has been invaluable. There are many others whose writing has kept speedway alive over the years, including Tom Stenner, Eric Linden, John Chaplin, Maurice Jones and Martin Rogers as well as the editors, writers and photographers on all the speedway magazines, especially the *Speedway Star*.

Alf Medcalf recorded the fastest lap of the day at Britain's first ever speedway meeting.

Introduction

Although claims have been put forward for Camberley in Surrey and Droylesden in Lancashire as the original home of speedway in Great Britain, it is now generally accepted that the first real speedway meeting in this country took place at High Beech in Essex on 19 February 1928 at the back of the King's Oak Hotel.

The event was originally planned for 9 November 1927 but the ACU (Auto Cycle Union) would not sanction a meeting on a Sunday. After some persuasion however, Jack Hill-Bailey, secretary of the Ilford Motorcycle Club, working in concert with the Colchester Motorcycle Club, eventually obtained permission for a Sunday meeting.

After some distinctly wintry weather during the preceding week, with snow actually falling in the area, 19 February itself dawned bright and clear as riders, officials and spectators made their way to the newly constructed dirt track tucked away in Epping Forest. The organisers planned for an expected audience of around 3,000 visitors, who they intended should watch the racing from the centre green. In the event the spectators numbered more in the region of 30,000 and completely overwhelmed the marshals, who had to make hasty arrangements to accommodate them around the outside of the circuit as well as inside. The more enterprising spectators climbed up nearby trees and watched from the overhanging branches!

Speedway had most definitely arrived in this country. The *Motorcycle* magazine at the time said: 'A day's sport such as has never been seen in England was provided for the thousands who thronged the King's Oak Speedway, near Loughton, last Sunday … there was thrill upon thrill from 10.30 a.m. to 5.00 p.m.'

Under Johnnie Hoskins, speedway had first seen the light of day just over four years previously in Australia so, unsurprisingly, the leading riders of the day were Australian. Two of them, Billy Galloway and Keith MacKay, were present at High Beech. However, they did not have it all their own way as in the first solo event, which was run over five laps, British rider Alf Foulds managed to beat Galloway into second place.

Alf Medcalf, whose father owned a motorcycle shop in Colchester and who had been riding motorcycles ever since he could remember, was also present at that first meeting. Alf was often seen practising on his 'Duggie' on Lowestoft seafront for hours on end and by the early 1920s had become one of the leading racers and hill-climbers in East Anglia. On 19 February, Alf took his Douglas along to High Beech to see what all the fuss was about and came away with a cup which read, 'Awarded for the fastest lap – First British Dirt Track Races – High Beech, 19th February 1928'. Alf's fastest lap of the day was 26.8 seconds from a standing start. In spite of a speedway career that was to take him to Harringay, Wimbledon and White City, that cup was to remain Alf's most treasured possession.

This was a very early indication of the leading role East Anglia was to play in the history of speedway.

One
Norwich

The start of the mile scratch race in the first ever meeting in East Anglia on 17 August 1930. On the left is G. Middleton riding a bike with the hooter still attached. On the far side the rider, J. Newlands, is the only one wearing leathers.

Following that first meeting at High Beech, speedway spread rapidly throughout the country. In the same year (1928), meetings were held at Greenford, Blackpool, Manchester, Crystal Palace, Stamford Bridge, Brighton, Swindon, Bradford, Burnley, Coventry, Edinburgh, Bolton, Rochdale, Leicester, Huddersfield and Cardiff (who opened on Boxing Day) to name but a few. Some tracks proved to be one-meeting wonders while others, like Manchester Belle Vue and Coventry, continued for many years.

East Anglia did not get in on the act until 1930, when grass track meetings were staged at the Firs Stadium in Holt Road, Norwich, under promoter Don Hannent on behalf of Eastern Speedways. It is generally accepted that the first meeting was held on 17 August 1930, although there are some unconfirmed references to a meeting being held at Easter of that year. A crowd of 5,000 turned up to see Fred Leavis from Cambridge take on established stars such as Bill Butler. A follow up meeting was held on 14 September 1930. Unfortunately, this meeting was held in the pouring rain and attracted only 1,000 spectators.

In 1931 there were regular meetings throughout the summer, with the first being held on 26 April in front of a 4,000 strong crowd. The biggest crowd of the season, almost 6,000, came to see the meeting on 12 July. This figure was almost repeated on 30 August when three new riders – Johnny Bull, who was alleged to weigh sixteen stone, Bert Linn and Herb Peters – made their way to Norwich from London. It was at this meeting that the Eastern Motor Club Ltd made the announcement that preparations were in hand to turn the track in to a dirt track.

The very first genuine dirt track speedway meeting to take place in East Anglia was, therefore, on 13 September 1931 when Norwich took on a team calling itself Staines. By this time league racing had been introduced into Great Britain with two leagues, the Southern League and the Northern League, forming the backbone of speedway racing in this country. Spectators had quickly got tired of the meaningless scratch races that had formed the programme for meetings and wanted to be able to cheer on their favourite local riders in more meaningful competitions. So, although Norwich had not yet joined one of the leagues, they formed a team and raced a series of challenge matches, the first one being the match against Staines.

That very first Norwich team consisted of Arthur Reynolds (captain), George Francies (vice-captain), Herb Peters, Bert Linn, Johnny Bull, Joe Nelson and reserves Jack Williams, Les Warboys and Don Dimes.

In many cases riders did not use their real names. Because league racing had become the mainstay of speedway racing, clubs had signed up riders on exclusive contracts. To get round this restriction on their earning capacity, some of the riders took false names and rode freelance at non-league tracks such as Norwich. It is known for example that Arthur Reynolds was in reality Fred Leavis, Herb Peters was Bert Garrish and Jack Williams was Allen Kilfoyle, who had ridden for the original Stamford Bridge team.

Existing photographs of that initial dirt track meeting and first ever team match show at least two of the riders racing while wearing collars and ties! In fact the whole atmosphere of speedway racing at this time in Norwich was very relaxed, with riders riding in whatever clothes they felt like – there is even a photograph of one rider apparently smoking a cigarette while racing! The track announcer did his commentating from a bus, which he drove home after the meeting, and there were of course no automatic starting gates; all races got underway with a rolling start. The bikes were not yet specialised; they were mostly stripped down road

Two leading riders in the early days of Norwich were Arthur Reynolds (real name Fred Leavis) and Geoff Pymar. Reynolds has a speedometer on his bike.

machines and a variety of makes could be seen, such as Douglas, Rudge-Whitworth, Triumph and Norton.

On 4 October 1931, Norwich took on a team calling itself Cambridge. This time, Jack Smythe was included in the Norwich team. Jack Smythe's real name was Jack Sharpe, one of the top names of the early 1930s, who later rode for Australia in Test matches.

As the 1931 season drew to a close, plans were drawn up to create a banked track with a new safety fence to replicate the Crystal Palace, one of the leading stadiums in the country at that time. A grandstand was also planned, although in the event this was not quite ready for the opening match of the 1932 season – Norwich versus London – but was completed in time for the second match on 10 April. Jack Smythe continued to dominate proceedings at Norwich, but on 1 May 1932 a new rider, Geoff Pymar, was brought into the Norwich team against Lea Bridge. Pymar, twenty years old and originally from Eye in Suffolk, had already ridden at Norwich. In fact he had gone along to the first ever meeting but was unable to get a ride, though he did manage to ride in the second meeting – but this was the first time he had been included in the team. In the following meeting he broke the track record.

Pymar's exploits brought him to the attention of the Wimbledon manager, J.R. Cory, who offered him a trial. Although a little out of his depth at first, he quickly learnt and was taken under the wing of the great Vic Huxley, arguably the top rider of this period, and became his partner in the Wimbledon team. Eventually, Pymar went on to ride in six Test matches for England against Australia and even made the World Championship final in 1938. After the war he rode for a number of teams, returning to Norwich in 1956 and Yarmouth in 1960. He eventually retired at the end of the 1962 season, having had one of the longest careers in speedway history.

Geoff Pymar, complete with collar and tie but no gloves, rides his AJS at Norwich in 1930.

By the middle of 1932, crowds had settled down to a regular 5,000 and other local venues began to appear on the grass track scene. A meeting was held at Lowestoft Road, Oulton Broad, on 9 April 1932, which was run by Lowestoft and District Speedway. Eleven meetings were held at Doles Meadow, Bradwell, run by Waveney Speed Track, who also ran one at Crown Meadow, Lowestoft, on 13 August 1932. Two meetings were held at the greyhound track in Caister Road, Yarmouth, two at Fakenham and yet another at Downham Market on 14 July 1932.

On 17 July 1932, Norwich entertained Staines again, who then went on to race at Yarmouth in the evening. The Yarmouth track was on a site to the south of where the 'Bloaters' were later to race after the war. Greyhound racing also started at the Firs in 1932, with meetings held on Mondays, Thursdays and Saturdays, and speedway on Sundays.

Racing continued in this vein for a while, but gradually the top riders stopped coming, even with their assumed names, as their parent tracks began to tighten up. By 1935 racing had come to a complete halt at Norwich with only one meeting, on Easter Sunday, being held. Pakefield took over the dirt track licence and ran a number of meetings during that season, including matches with a team called Lowestoft racing against 'London' and Hackney Wick. In 1936 several meetings were again organised at Pakefield, which was known as 'The Track by the Silver Sea'.

Norwich staged one meeting in 1936. This was when Putt Mossman's Motorcycle Rodeo and Circus came to town. Putt Mossman was a Californian who had got together a team of speedway riders – including Pee Wee Cullum and the Mexican Manual Trujillo – to tour the world, racing against teams, but also putting on stunt performances. In 1936 they toured Great Britain and raced against a number of Provincial League clubs. It was said that the crowds they pulled in helped save Southampton, Cardiff, Nottingham, Plymouth,

Bristol and Liverpool from extinction. Mossman's speciality was to race blindfolded up an inclined plank and jump his Harley Davidson machine over his wife, Helen, as she lay on the ground!

Speedway returned to Norwich with a vengeance in 1937. Max Grosskreutz of Belle Vue and Australia, one of the leading riders of the early 1930s, decided to inject life into Norwich and to open it up as a proper league team. Max had had an excellent 1936 and was thought by many to be the top rider of the year. Unfortunately, injury had disrupted his season and he had had to withdraw from the first ever World Championship. However, a few days after Lionel Van Praag became the first world champion, Max Grosskreutz defeated him in a race and, just as it seemed that the speedway world was at his feet, Max surprised everyone with the shock announcement of his retirement. The Harringay management, thinking Max was merely wishing to leave Belle Vue, offered £7,000 for his services – a record transfer fee at that time – but the offer was rejected.

Instead, Grosskreutz decided to go into management and to enter Norwich for the Provincial League. In 1932 the old Northern and Southern Leagues had been amalgamated to form the National League and in 1936 a new Provincial League (in effect a second division) had been started. Grosskreutz laid a completely new cinder track and made various other improvements to the stadium. He also declared that he was to be the team's chief coach and mechanic and, as if that wasn't enough, he also built all the team's bikes!

Programme cover from the meeting held at the Firs on 4 September 1932.

Norwich's first league team consisted of Dick Wise as captain, Wilf Jay, Chum Moore, Jim Millward, Bill Birtwell and Jock Sweet. The side was later strengthened by the inclusion of Wal Morton and Max's fellow Australian, the spectacular leg-trailing Bert Spencer. A young Malcolm Craven, later to find fame with West Ham, also rode in four matches for the Norwich Stars but was rejected as not being good enough.

By the end of the season, Norwich were attracting crowds of 9,000 on a regular basis and with those fans in mind Max Grosskreutz declared: 'I honestly believe there is no body of supporters so loyal and enthusiastic in any sport as speedway followers. The number of "regulars" occupying the same seats or stands week after week is a source of gratification to all speedway managers, apart from financial considerations.'

There was to be no fairy tale end to the season, however, as initially Norwich found it a bit of a struggle and finished fifth out of six teams, winning only eight out of twenty matches.

Nevertheless, Grosskreutz was determined that speedway would continue at Norwich and that 1938 would see a big improvement. Just before the new season started he said: 'The crowd shall have their money's worth. They want thrills; I shall see that they get them. They want Norwich to be the best team in the provinces – well, I'll try to make them that too.' He was urged to make a riding comeback, but insisted that 'promoting is a full-time job' and that he would concentrate on coaching 'his boys'. Further improvements were made to the stadium in an effort to improve the attendance figures to at least 10,000.

In the event, the urge to return to active riding proved too strong to resist and when Bert Spencer was recalled by his parent club Wimbledon, Max decided it was time to help his team

Norwich Stars, 1937. From left to right: Jock Sweet, Alec Peel, McMahon (promoter), Max Grosskreutz (manager), Dick Wise (captain, on bike), Wilf Jay, Paul Goodchild, Bill Birtwell, Bert Spencer.

Left: *Dick Wise first rode at Norwich in the pioneering days of the early 1930s before becoming captain of the 1937/38 league team and then manager after the war.* Right: *Max Grosskreutz in 1937, the year he brought league speedway to Norwich.*

out. Many in speedway thought that a man of his class should be banned from the Second Division (which the Provincial League had now been officially renamed), but there was no rule about it and so Grosskreutz returned to the saddle. Not forgetting his role as manager and coach, Grosskreutz declared that as soon as Norwich had scored enough points in any match to be sure of winning he would withdraw and allow the reserves to take his place, thus giving them more experience. In his first match he scored a maximum, showing that he had lost none of his old flair. His inspiration proved to be just the tonic Norwich needed. Not only did Norwich finish second in the League, but they also caused a sensation by beating First Division Harringay in the National Trophy. At that time the Harringay team included some of the leading riders in the country, including Jack and Norman Parker, Alec Statham, Jack Ormston and Les Wotton. Grosskreutz, of course, scored a maximum.

As for the League title, Norwich finished the season level on points with Hackney Wick, but Hackney Wick were declared the winners by virtue of having scored more race points through the season. Norwich fans still feel strongly to this day that they were robbed of the title because if the decision had been taken in the normal way of points average they would have won, as they finished with an average of 1.34 to Hackney's 1.32. As the season had approached its end and it became obvious that the league title hung in the balance, Hackney

Left: Paul Goodchild rode for Norwich in all three pre-war seasons. Right: The programme cover for the Leeds versus Norwich Second Division match on 23 July 1938. True to his word, Grosskreutz withdrew from his last race in favour of reserve Syd Littlewood, having won his first three and ensured Norwich's victory by 52 points to 29.

Wick had offered to race Norwich for the title over two legs – on condition that Grosskreutz was excluded from the Norwich team. The offer was rejected.

The Norwich team which had brought its share of glory to East Anglia consisted of Dick Wise (captain), Max Grosskreutz, Bill Birtwell, Alan Smith, Wilf Jay, Jock Sweet, Paul Goodchild and Syd Littlewood. Bert Spencer also returned to Norwich later in the season.

On an individual level, Max Grosskreutz had a very successful season, leading Australia to a surprise victory over England in the first Test match at Belle Vue. Watched by 40,000 spectators, he top scored for the Kangaroos with 15 points. Incidentally, the attendance at the Test match was nothing out of the ordinary for speedway at that time. A massive crowd of 93,000 watched the World Championship final at Wembley in 1938 and a total of 4,081,262 people passed through the turnstiles at all matches during the season. Norwich were watched by 205,777 of these.

With the return of Wal Morton and Bert Spencer for the 1939 season, Max Grosskreutz once again decided to call it a day and retired from riding, concentrating on his promotional and managerial activities. As the season started he stated: 'I certainly think we shall lift the Second Division Championship this year. Remember it was only mathematics, not loss of form, which beat us last November.' Grosskreutz had also been talent-spotting and signed up Albert Hutson (aged nineteen) and Sid Hipperson (twenty-five), who he had seen at the Horsford amateur track. Of course, Norwich were not destined to win the Second Division title, but then nor was any other team as in September the outbreak of war put a stop to all competitive speedway in this country.

Only Belle Vue managed to keep speedway racing going throughout the wartime years. Along with the rest of the country's tracks, Norwich's activities were suspended for the duration. However, in 1946 the sport roared back into action stronger than ever as two leagues, the National League and the Northern League, were formed. Norwich found themselves in the Northern League alongside Middlesbrough, Sheffield, Birmingham, Newcastle and Glasgow.

Max Grosskreutz had long since departed these shores and it was left to Dick Wise, the pre-war captain, to take over the reins of management at Norwich. Because of the intervention of war, the Speedway Control Board felt the fairest way to start the new season was for all riders to be pooled and then allocated on an equitable basis so that no team would be too strong. All teams were allowed to pick two riders from their pre-war team before the allocation began. Norwich chose to keep Wal Morton and Wilf Jay. However, before the season started Bert Spencer, who had been allocated to Glasgow, asked if he could stay at Norwich and Dick Wise agreed to swap him for Wal Morton. Thus the allocated starting line-up for 1946 was Bert Spencer, Wilf Jay, Ted Bravery, Paddy Mills, Sid Hipperson, Geoff Dykes, Albert Hutson and

Wal Morton, pictured in Norwich's colours in 1939. He returned to Norwich in 1948 and 1957 and continued riding until well into the 1960s.

NOT TRANSFERABLE

NORWICH SPEEDWAY SUPPORTERS CLUB, 1949

H. A. Tooley, Hon. Sec., 32 Links Avenue, Reepham Rd, Norwich.

Tel. : HELLESDON 315

MEMBER'S TICKET

No. 1404

Name Mr. a. King

Address 13, TRAFFORD ROAD NORWICH.

Attention is drawn to Rules and Bye-laws contained in your Rule Book, particularly to Rule 18 and Bye-laws No. 14 and 15.

A Norwich Supporters' Club card dating from 1949. Crowds of over 20,000 were not unknown at Norwich in the late 1940s, with one meeting in 1947 attracting 26,000.

Keith Harvey. Some more pre-season shuffling saw Dykes and Harvey leave the team and Don Houghton and Harwood Pike brought in. During the season more riders were brought into the team, including Roy Duke, Len Read, Jack 'Bluey' Thorpe and Paddy Hammond.

All riders were graded into five ranks, with grade one riders earning 30 shillings (£1.50) a start and 30 shillings a point, and the lowest grade getting 10 shillings a start and 10 shillings a point. Norwich's top graded rider was Bert Spencer, who was graded in the third rank, earning 20 shillings a start and 20 shillings a point.

The 1946 season proved to be the start of a bumper period for speedway, when it almost rivalled football as the country's national sport. Norwich's total gate for the year more than doubled from 205,777 in 1938 to 436,222 in 1946, with average attendances at almost 20,000. Considering the ground capacity was only 24,000, this was good going. The track itself was 425 yards long, one of the longest in the league.

The Stars had an average year finishing third out of six and going out in the first preliminary round of the National Trophy to Birmingham. Their biggest success was to win the Northern Trophy, beating Sheffield in the final by 106-85, and also the ACU Cup (Northern).

The undoubted star of Norwich's first post-war season was skipper, Bert Spencer, still leg-trailing when most of the rest of the world had long since abandoned this form of broadsiding in favour of the foot forward style. Bert finished the season top of the averages and top point-scorer, not only for Norwich but also in the whole of the Northern League with 200 points from 20 matches. He also qualified for the Riders' Championship final, held that year in place of the World Championship, where he scored 5 points and came tenth.

Bert began his speedway career in Queensland, Australia, in 1925 at the age of seventeen. After coming over to this country in 1928, he joined Exeter. In 1930 he transferred to Leicester and then to Plymouth. In 1935 he joined Wimbledon, who loaned him out to the newly formed Norwich Stars in 1937. Apart from a recall to his parent club Wimbledon for a short period in 1938, Spencer was to stay at Norwich for the rest of his career in this country. In 1938, he rode for Australia in a series of Second Division Test matches, England versus the Dominions. The first Test was held at Newcastle and Bert not only scored 17 out of a possible 18 points, but also broke the track record.

Wilf Jay also proved to be one of the Northern League's top riders, scoring 166 points, but perhaps the most satisfying performance of all came from Paddy Mills. Before the war, Paddy had been regarded as something of a joke on the speedway. No track would take him as a team member, though eventually Bluey Wilkinson gave him a run at Sheffield. After the war, Mills was allocated to Norwich and became a revelation. He scored 153 points in 1946 to claim the third heat leader spot and was, in fact, the eleventh highest scorer in the whole of the Northern League. By the following season, he had become Norwich's top scorer, a position he was to maintain in 1948.

At the end of the season, Wilf Jay and Don Houghton were swapped for Newcastle's Syd Littlewood, who lived in Norwich and had therefore asked for a transfer. Wilf's move brought

Left: *Ted Bravery, who rode for Norwich between 1946 and 1950, was a consistent points scorer and first-class team man.* Right: *Paddy Mills was Norwich's top scorer from 1947 to 1949.*

Norwich's captain, Bert Spencer, in spectacular leg-trailing action as he sweeps past Gil Craven of Cradley Heath in 1949.

Wilf Jay was brought to Norwich by Max Grosskreutz in 1937 and stayed until 1946. He won his first and last races for the club.

OWING TO INJURY TO HIS LEFT KNEE OUR WORTHY CAPTAIN BERT SPENCER IS LIKELY TO BE OUT OF ACTION FOR SOME WEEKS — BUT WE CAN RELY UPON HIS MORAL SUPPORT FOR OUR GALLANT TEAM OF 'STARS WHO ARE SURE TO DO SOME FINE RIDING — HEADED BY PADDY MILLS AND TED BRAVERY.

E.H.BANGER '47.

A cartoon that appeared in the Norwich programme the week after Bert Spencer's injury in 1947.

to an end a nine-year association with the club. He had originally been spotted by Max Grosskreutz in 1936 at Belle Vue and when he opened Norwich, Grosskreutz brought Jay with him. He became an overnight sensation, winning his first race and three further races during the evening. He also won his last race for Norwich in 1946. Later on he was to hold the Division Two Match Race title, beating Fred Tuck.

The following year dawned with the Norwich line-up consisting of Bert Spencer, Ted Bravery, Paddy Mills, Roy Duke, Don Houghton, Sid Hipperson, Len Read, Bluey Thorpe, Charlie Challis, Paddy Hammond, Jack Freeman, Geoff Revett and Syd Littlewood. Because of the amazing success of speedway in 1946, eleven more teams had applied to join the league in 1947. This had now been reorganised into the National League Divisions One, Two and Three. Norwich were in Division Two.

Norwich were unlucky when Bert Spencer was injured and missed a number of matches. This did bring some good fortune though, as the replacement brought in for Spencer was a young Phil Clarke, who quickly established himself in the team and was destined to become one of Norwich's leading riders. He went on to stay with the Stars for a further twelve years, until 1959. However, it did mean that Norwich were once again to miss out on league honours finishing the season in third place behind Middlesbrough and Sheffield. Although he eventually missed out on eleven matches, Spencer was still Norwich's second highest scorer behind Mills, with Ted Bravery in third place.

The team announced to start the 1948 season differed very little from that which had finished 1947, however there had been some alterations to the stadium itself. As the sport was still growing in popularity – some 460,000 had passed through the turnstiles in 1947 – the accommodation had been extended to hold 26,000. There were also three supporters' clubrooms where dances were held on Tuesdays, Thursdays and Saturdays throughout the season. Race night continued to be on Saturdays.

Gates were still increasing but once again, owing to injury, Norwich were to miss out on league and cup honours. For the second year running Bert Spencer was injured and missed a number of crucial meetings. Aussie Powell also missed the last two months of the season with a broken bone in his leg and although Paddy Mills did his best and Phil Clarke continued to improve, Norwich did not have the depth in strength to see them through. Ted Bravery, who announced early in the season that this was to be his last, and Geoff Revett were inconsistent while Jack Freeman and Syd Littlewood were not up to their previous best. Although they reached the Division Two final of the National Trophy, further progress was thwarted by

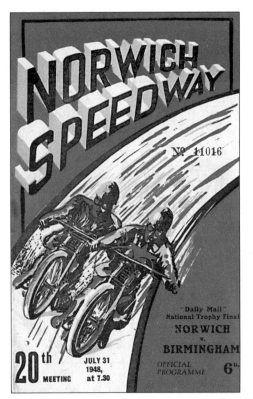

Left: *The programme for the 1948 National Trophy final, which was won by Birmingham.* Right: *Aussie Powell began his career at Dagenham in 1936 and came to Norwich in 1947. He proved to be a good trainer of young riders and brought on many riders such as Pat Clarke and Jack Unstead.*

Norwich's bogey team, Birmingham, who won both legs. Birmingham also inflicted a home defeat on Norwich in the league.

The final league placing was even more disappointing, as Norwich finished in fifth place out of nine. In spite of this, however, Norwich applied to join the First Division along with Birmingham. Birmingham were accepted, but Norwich's application was rejected, owing to 'difficulties over raising teams'. On an individual note, Dick Wise did receive a personal honour when he was chosen by the Australian Auto Cycle Union to be one of their Test selectors along with Bill Longley and A.E. Simcock.

Although 1948 was generally a good year for speedway in East Anglia, with new tracks at Yarmouth and Rayleigh and attendances up at Norwich, the sport was beginning to feel the first effects of the new government Entertainment Tax, which was pushing up the price of admission. It was calculated that 58 per cent of gate money went to the exchequer in tax, including 48 per cent on Entertainment Tax. On 7 April the Control Board decided to appeal to the Chancellor of the Exchequer against the budget decision not to grant speedway a reduction in Entertainment Tax. The Treasury had declared, somewhat incredibly, that 'speedway is not a live sport, therefore it does not qualify for an income tax rebate'! The appeal fell on deaf ears and speedway continued to pay the Entertainment Tax.

Right from the start of the 1949 season, it was apparent that only one team would dominate Division Two and, unfortunately, that team was not Norwich! The journalist Len Simpson summed it up when he said: 'From the campaign opening a mere matter of weeks sufficed to make it depressingly obvious that Bristol would romp home alone.' It was also abundantly clear that, after Bristol, the two top teams in Division Two would be Sheffield and Norwich. Consequently, the only spark of interest in the season came when Sheffield and Norwich met, with each winning on the other's home track. Unfortunately, although Norwich managed to beat Bristol at home twice, they lost to Cradley Heath and finished the season in third place. Apart from these two home defeats, Norwich rattled up some stunning victories as they disposed of Coventry 67-16 and 62-22, Newcastle 63-21 and 59-24 and Southampton 61-23 twice.

As well as finishing third in the league, Norwich also reached the Second Division final of the National Trophy, losing to Bristol by 111-105. Phil Clarke scored an 18-point maximum in the second leg at Norwich, which they won by 76 points to 32, having lost the first leg by 79 points to 29.

Paddy Mills was again Norwich's top scorer for the season and was rated fifth best rider in the division as a whole. He started off the season like an express train, scoring seven maximums from eight matches. He was even selected as reserve for the second Test at Birmingham, but was unfortunately injured a few days before and unable to take his place. Mills had in fact asked for a transfer over the close season as he felt he would like to get into the top division. Norwich offered to sell him to Harringay for £1,500 plus two juniors, but Harringay said they were 'not very interested'.

Mills was joined in the top ten rankings by Phil Clarke, who also won the Division Two Match Race Championship from Bristol's Billy Hole and new Australian sensation, Bob Leverenz. He finished his first season in this country with 293 points at an average of 6.97 and caused a major upset when he won the Norwich round of the World Championship. Bert Spencer was once again injured and at the end of the season decided that he had had enough

Jack Freeman rode for Norwich from 1947 to 1952.

and went into semi-retirement. He continued to race in Australia, but did not reappear in England. Of the other riders, Ted Bravery (who hadn't retired at the end of the 1948 season after all), Fred Rogers and Syd Littlewood all had fairly moderate seasons, each averaging just over 5 points per match, while Jack Freeman scored 4.56 per match.

It was Jack Freeman, however, who saved Norwich even more embarrassment when, in an end of season challenge match, Yarmouth defeated the Stars by 56 to 28. Only Freeman with seven points and a bonus managed to contain the rampant Bloaters.

With Bristol promoted to Division One, the Second Division took on a more competitive nature. Even up to the last week of the 1950 season any one of four or five teams could have snatched the title. The fact that it was Norwich who finally came through was a tribute to the hard work put in by the management and riders and the dedicated support of the fans.

Dick Wise had retired at the end of the previous season and the new manager at Norwich was Fred Evans, whose previous experience of speedway had been as Hackney Wick's manager. The retirement of Dick Wise and Bert Spencer had severed the last links with the early days of Norwich's league team and left them ready to enter the second half of the twentieth century with a new look as new riders now began to take over from the more established stars. Phil Clarke topped the team's averages with 9.28 and Bob Leverenz followed him on 8.25. Fred Rogers and Johnnie Davies had much improved seasons. Of the older names, Paddy Mills was still there at the top, but the still not yet retired Ted Bravery's average had dropped to 3.71 and Syd Littlewood's to 1.97.

Following in the tradition of Birmingham in 1948 and Bristol in 1949, Norwich applied for, and expected, promotion to Division One. However, it was not to be as the Division One promoters and the Control Board refused to sanction the request.

As 1951 dawned there was great unease in the speedway world. The final figures for 1950 revealed a 20 per cent drop in attendances. Many reasons were put forward including, of course, the Entertainment Tax as well as the inability of promoters and the Control Board to settle plans for the season until a week or so before the start. The sport had received hostile national press because the Control Board had turned down Norwich's application to join Division One and because it had demoted Plymouth from Division Two to Division Three, even though they had finished ninth out of fifteen. The reason given was the cost of travelling involved for other clubs in the division.

The opposition to Norwich's promotion had come from the London tracks, who said that past experience with Birmingham and Bristol showed that they were strong at home and weak away and therefore no attraction when visiting the London teams who made up the majority of the league. When it was put to the vote the five London clubs, Harringay, New Cross, Wembley, West Ham and Wimbledon, outvoted the others, Birmingham, Belle Vue, Bradford and Bristol, and poor old Norwich were consigned to another year in Division Two.

Norwich proved just what a farce the decision not to promote them was by romping away with the League title by a clear ten points, as well as becoming the first Second Division team since the war to beat First Division opposition in the National Trophy, when they defeated

The 1950 Norwich team that won the Second Division. From left to right, back row: Alex Hunter, Syd Littlewood, Fred Evans (manager), Fred Rogers, Bob Leverenz, Jack Freeman. Front row: F. Wilson (deputy manager), Johnny Davies, Paddy Mills, Phil Clarke.

25

Bristol by 109 points to 107. Norwich stood head and shoulders above the opposition. At home they went through the season unbeaten while away they lost just six matches out of thirty. Fred Evans' declared policy at the beginning of the season had been that if the London promoters would not let them into the First Division, 'we'll smash our way in'. His policy of ruthlessly flattening all opposition at last paid off as Norwich were finally promoted at the end of the season.

The team had a very solid look about it, with even the seventh man, Fred Pawson, recording an average of 5.93 for the season. Above him, Bob Leverenz was the undoubted star, scoring 282 points in 28 matches. Leverenz qualified for the World Championship final, where he scored 7 points and finished in ninth place. This would have been the best placing by a Second Division rider in the history of the World Championship had it not been for the fact that in the same year Jack Young of Edinburgh actually became the only Second Division rider ever to win the World Championship. Leverenz was also selected to ride for Australia in all five Test matches that season.

Phil Clarke was as reliable as ever, averaging 8.44, while Fred Rogers recorded 6.76 and newcomer, Alec Hunter from Australia, scored 6.58. Paddy Mills, although not the force he once was, still weighed in with a more than useful 6.03, while Jack Freeman finished on 5.96. Norwich had proved themselves far too good for Second Division opposition and were now looking forward to taking on the top teams and the top riders in the country.

In spite of problems on the economic front, speedway in East Anglia was looking forward to a boom era. With Norwich now at last in the First Division, the region was represented in

Left: *Alex Hunter was a member of the Norwich team between 1949 and 1953.* Right: *Bob Leverenz was ninth in the 1951 World Championship.*

Left: *A programme cover from the 1951 Kemsley Trophy match against Oxford on 12 May.* Right: *A selection of Norwich ephemera from the 1950s and '60s.*

all three leagues and with the formation of Ipswich, the possibility of an Eastern Cup, the long-cherished idea of Yarmouth promoter, E.H. Wedon, came one step nearer.

Unfortunately, Norwich's high hopes for 1952 were not to be fulfilled. In a disastrous season in which all but one of the team suffered injury at some time or another, they finished bottom of the league with just one away win to their credit and were knocked out of the National Trophy by Second Division Poole. Even taking into account the injuries it was apparent that Norwich were not First Division material and proved to be the weakest team to enter the First Division since the war. After the fight they had had to get in the league it was a great disappointment and just reaffirmed the belief of some that promotion should not be automatic.

The only bit of good luck Norwich enjoyed was the signing of Bill Gilbert. Gilbert came into prominence in 1948 when, after three seasons with Wembley, he was chosen for England in the fourth Test match and scored 13 points. He then went on to take fourth place in the Riders' Championship of that year. In 1949 he was Wembley's top scorer with 357 points, but at the end of the 1950 season he retired. With Norwich short of star material, Fred Evans approached Wembley and asked if they would release him. Wembley's reply was to the effect that, 'if you can persuade him to come out of retirement you can have him!' Evans proved to be very persuasive and Gilbert signed on the dotted line in time for the start of the season. By the end of the season he was the only Norwich

Left: *Bill Gilbert had just one season with Norwich (in 1952) but finished it as top scorer.* Right: *Aub Lawson, one of the greatest riders of all time, and an automatic choice for Australia.*

rider not to have been injured and to have appeared in every match. He was also the Stars' top scorer.

Of the rest of the team only Bob Leverenz was able to show that he was capable of mixing it with the best in Division One. He finished with a ten-point average, one of only three riders in the whole division to do so, the others being current World Champion, Jack Young, and future World Champion, Ronnie Moore. Leverenz was in good company! Unfortunately, he only took part in seventeen matches and left for Australia and home in mid-season. One other bright spot was the return of Yarmouth's Billy Bales from National Service. Promoted to the Norwich side, he scored 188 points in 26 matches at an average of 7.2. Of the rest Paddy Mills, in what was to be his last season with Norwich, scored a miserable 43 points in 17 matches, while even Phil Clarke found the going tough, finishing the season with an average score of just 3.7. Just as Norwich thought things couldn't get any worse, both Bob Leverenz and Bill Gilbert announced their retirement at the end of the season.

The speedway world was full of optimism for the start of the 1953 season. Although crowds were no longer reaching the numbers attained in the immediate post-war years, the sport had nevertheless settled down with a strong core of support and three healthy divisions supporting a total of twenty-six teams, of which four were in East Anglia. Even the Control Board seemed to have got its act together and had planned an attractive programme for Coronation year, with a completely revamped National Trophy, giving teams in the lower divisions more chance of winning through to the later rounds and meeting the 'big boys'.

Unfortunately, the reality of the 1953 season was somewhat different as the Coronation and an extremely wet summer combined to keep the crowds away. The biggest shock of the season came when one of the leading London clubs, New Cross, closed down in mid-season at a time when they were pressing Harringay hard for the leadership of the Coronation Cup table, a special event introduced for that year. The demise of New Cross sent shivers down the spines of all promoters throughout the country. If it could happen to such a prominent team as New Cross then it could happen to anyone.

Norwich were already in trouble before the season even started. Bottom of the league in 1952 and with their two best riders gone, Norwich were facing a very uncertain future. Fortunately, they were able to entice Aub Lawson back into league racing after a season's absence. Lawson, an Australian from New South Wales, first rode in England in 1939, when he was signed by Wembley. He qualified for the World Championship final that year, though it was never held due to the outbreak of war. On his return to this country in 1947, he linked up with West Ham and became one of the very top names in the sport, achieving second place in the 1949 world rankings behind Jack Parker and third place in 1950 and 1951. In 1950 Lawson became the first rider to beat Jack Parker for the British Match Race title since 1947. Parker had been so dominant in the event that it had become known as Parker's Pension.

Lawson had retired at the end of 1951 and was not able to recapture his world-class form during 1953. *Stenner's Annual* (the bible of speedway racing in the early 1950s) even dismissed him as a 'declining star'. This was far from the truth, but unfortunately it appeared this way in 1953, even though he did reach the World Championship final and finished in ninth place with 7 points. Norwich were able to profit from New Cross' demise by signing up Cyril Roger, but he arrived too late to breathe life into the declining fortune of the Stars and, indeed, never recaptured his New Cross form anyway, finishing the season with a very mediocre 6.6 average. As for the rest of the team they found it very hard going as even Billy Bales only managed an average of 5.0, while Phil Clarke scored just 78 points in 16 matches. Alec Hunter had a disastrous season, scoring a mere 9 points from 10 matches, less than a point a match!

Norwich finished the season with just 12 points from sixteen matches: the points coming from six home wins. Incredibly, two teams finished below them in the league: the once mighty Belle Vue managed only 11 points, while Bristol took the wooden spoon with 10.

The closure of New Cross presaged the beginning of a dramatic decline in the fortunes of speedway, which continued until the end of the decade. The 1954 season started with only twenty teams as opposed to the twenty-eight that had started the previous year. The Southern League was disbanded and the remaining teams joined the Second Division, so that there were now only two major leagues, although a new training league for novices, the Metropolitan League, did come into being.

The 1953 season had also seen the last of the classic England versus Australia Test match encounters, with their place being taken by England versus Australasia contests. Statistics at the end of the series showed that the former Norwich star, Max Grosskreutz, had appeared in 44 Test matches, the third highest of any rider behind Ron Johnson (55) and Jack Parker (52), and was Australia's top points scorer with 374 points, second only to England's Jack Parker who had scored 460. Aub Lawson had made 28 appearances scoring 164 points.

Although storm clouds were on the horizon, both for the general future of speedway and for the future of speedway in East Anglia in particular, Norwich turned in their best performance for some years in 1954. They finished fourth in the league and reached the final of the National Trophy, where they lost to Wembley by 123 points to 92. One reason for this improvement was the arrival of former Wembley rider and world number three, Bob Oakley. Aub Lawson was returning to something like his best form, although he did not have one of his best years in the World Championship final, scoring only 4 points and finishing in fourteenth position, just ahead of Peter Craven and Sweden's Ove Fundin who occupied the last two places.

Ove Fundin had in fact won through to the final as runner-up to Aub Lawson in the Norwich round of the World Championship, scoring 13 points on a bike tied up with bits of old wire and string. When he arrived at Wembley for the final he still had just this one bike and no mechanic. Lawson arranged for a mechanic to help him, but it was hard going as Fundin could speak no English and the mechanic could not speak any Swedish! Aub Lawson had, however, seen the enormous potential in this youngster from Tranas and when Fundin again performed well during a tour of Australia in the close season, Lawson recommended to new Norwich manager Gordon Parkins that Fundin be snapped up before anyone else signed him.

Norwich started the 1955 season without Fred Rogers (who had left for Belle Vue) for the first time since 1948. Fred had been born in Norwich in 1929 and was a protégé of Paddy Mills; he finished second in his very first competitive race. Before settling at Norwich, Fred had ridden at Sheffield, Bradford and Newcastle, returning to the Norwich/Yarmouth set up in 1948. He had always been a good solid team man, without setting the world alight, averaging around the 6-point mark year in and year out. His place was taken by Harry Edwards, formerly of Walthamstow and Belle Vue, and brother of Ipswich's Bert.

The 1954 Norwich team. From left to right, back row: Fred Brand, Bob Oakley, Fred Evans (manager), Cyril Roger, Fred Rogers. Front row: Billy Bales, Phil Clarke, Merv Neil, Aub Lawson.

Harringay's Split Waterman leads Fred Rogers in 1954.

At the start of the season it seemed as though Norwich would carry on from where they left off and finish in the top half of the table, but injuries to Aub Lawson, who broke his collar bone twice during the season, soon put paid to that and Norwich finished just one point above West Ham at the foot of the table. Norwich did however come good in the National Trophy, winning the title for the first time in their history, reversing the previous year's result and beating the mighty Wembley in the final by 109 points to 106. Wembley were completely outridden in the first leg by a rampant Norwich who won the match by 21 points, with new boy Ove Fundin scoring 16. There was a welcome return to form by Billy Bales, who averaged over 10 for the season, while Fundin, who was drafted into the team late on, managed to score 73 points from just 6 matches.

On an individual level, Norwich riders did remarkably well in the World Championship. Ove Fundin, Phil Clarke, Cyril Roger and Aub Lawson all qualified for the final, with Fundin scoring 10 points and coming sixth. Aub Lawson's injury put him out of the final and his place was taken by yet another Norwich rider, Billy Bales. Phil Clarke, Cyril Roger and Billy Bales all represented England in the Test match series, Bales top scoring with 13 points in the last Test at Norwich while, in spite of his injuries, Aub Lawson managed to ride for Australasia in all six Tests.

Unfortunately, speedway's decline continued and the 1956 season started with yet another London club, West Ham, withdrawing from the League (Harringay had closed at the end of the 1954 season). The two divisions were down to a total of just fourteen tracks, seven in each division, from sixteen the previous year. Exeter were the other club to close its doors. To keep the numbers up in the First Division, Second Division champions Poole were promoted.

Changes to Norwich's line-up for 1956 included the departure of Cyril Roger and Don Lawson (Aub's stepbrother) and the arrival of Gerry Hussey, Reg Trott, Peter Atkins, Derek Strutt and Geoff Pymar, the man who had first ridden at the Firs Stadium back in 1930, and now a forty-four-year-old veteran. Gerry Hussey had arrived on the Division One scene with

Three of Norwich's greatest post-war stars: Aub Lawson, Ove Fundin and Billy Bales.

a bang back in 1953, scoring 7 points from the reserve berth in his first match for West Ham, but he never really made the very top grade, although he was always a good club rider. He scored 63 points from 10 matches for the Stars in 1956 and qualified for the World Final, where he came last with no points. Norwich favourite Phil Clarke again rode for England in the Test match series, as did Aub Lawson for Australasia.

However, 1956 was, of course, Ove Fundin's year. The young Swede had learnt his trade well and was now ready to take on the world. He had a ruthless determination to be World Champion and the courage and skill to match his ambition. For Norwich he rode in 19 matches scoring a total of 210 points, an average of 11.05. He won the Astorias' Trophy at Norwich, The Geoff Revett Cup at Ipswich, The Five Star Cup and Supporters' Trophy at Norwich and the C.T.S. Trophy at Norwich. In the first ever England versus Sweden Test series, Fundin started off with a maximum 18 points in the first Test, followed by scores of 11 and 15, helping Sweden to a sensational 3-0 series victory.

Fundin qualified for the World Championship final as winner of the European final in front of a 20,000 strong crowd in Oslo. The favourites for the World Final were Fundin himself, reigning champion Peter Craven, and 1954 champion, Ronnie Moore. When the draw was made it was discovered that all three riders had been drawn together in the opening heat along with another Swede, Per Olaf Soederman. As the opening ceremony and parade of riders finished the atmosphere in Wembley Stadium amongst the tens of thousands of spectators in the crowd and the riders in the pits became unbearably tense. It seemed almost certain that whoever won the opening heat would, in all probability, go on to win the title itself. Riding as only he knew how, the diminutive Wizard of Balance, Peter Craven, rode one of the most brilliant races of his career to completely dominate the others and take the chequered flag.

Two Norwich riders represent their countries in a Test match as Sweden's Ove Fundin takes England's Cyril Roger on the inside.

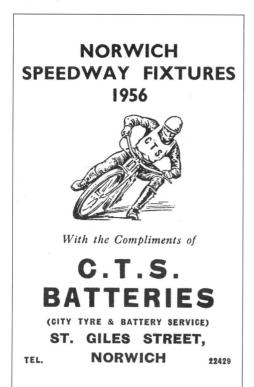

Left: *The front cover of Norwich's 1956 fixture list, showing that sponsorship is nothing new.* Right: *The front cover of the 1956 World Championship final programme.*

Ronnie Moore came second, with Fundin trailing in third. All the high hopes of the Swedish and Norwich contingents had received a shattering blow. However, Fundin was never one to panic. He remained cool and collected his thoughts as he sat in the pits waiting for his next ride. In his second ride, Craven was again off like a rocket and appeared an easy winner until disaster struck. He lost a valve on the fourth bend of the last lap and, although he managed to push home for third place, it meant the final was wide open again. Ronnie Moore dropped another point in his second ride, but Fundin made sure of victory in his, so that after two races the three of them were back on equal terms with four points each. In fact, the joint leaders at this stage were Barry Briggs and the unfancied Eric Boothroyd, both with five points.

Fundin won his third race, but Moore again came second, as did Craven who was now mounted on his second machine and unable to recapture the form shown in his first race. After three races, Fundin shared the lead with Brian Crutcher, Arthur Forrest and Ken McKinlay. McKinlay added another three points in his next race, while Forrest trailed in behind Ronnie Moore, who won his first race of the evening. Heat sixteen was another crucial race as it involved Fundin and Crutcher. It also turned out to be one of the most exciting of the evening as Fundin took the lead from the gate but was overtaken by Crutcher on the second lap riding round the outside. As Crutcher attempted to cross back to the white line he fell and the race was stopped. Crutcher was excluded and Fundin won the re-run.

With one more race to go each, five riders still had a chance of winning the title; Fundin and McKinlay had 10 points, followed by Moore, Briggs and Forrest on nine. McKinlay fell in his last race and in heat nineteen Moore defeated Crutcher, giving him a final total of 12 points.

Ove Fundin proudly holds the World Championship trophy after his first win in 1956. He went on to win it four more times.

The 1957 Norwich team. From left to right: Geoff Pymar, Phil Clarke, Harry Edwards, Gordon Parkins (manager), Aub Lawson, Ove Fundin, Wal Morton, Billy Bales. The mascot is John Lawson.

Just as you could feel the tension in the air before the first race, so you could feel the electricity in the atmosphere before the final race. If Fundin won it he would be World Champion, if he came second there would be a run-off. Facing Fundin in heat twenty was Arthur Forrest, who knew that if he could win he still had a chance of the world title.

Fundin's nerve held and he took the all important lead on the first bend. The Norwich supporters went wild with excitement, but Forrest wasn't finished yet. On the back straight of the second lap he shot by the Swedish rider on the outside, grabbing the lead and silencing the Norwich fans. It was the green and yellow scarves of the Stars' supporters who were to have the final laugh, however, as Fundin dived under Forrest on the next bend and retook the lead. This time he had no intention of giving it up and went on to win his first, Sweden's first and Norwich's first World Championship.

If he wasn't already, Fundin now became the hero of the Firs and remained that way until Norwich finally closed in 1964. In fact, amongst the Norwich supporters who still get together for their annual gathering to remember the good old days, he still is. *Speedway Star* readers can vote for Ivan Mauger as best rider of all time, but people in Norfolk know who the real rider of the millennium was!

As if the Entertainment Tax wasn't bad enough, speedway was struck by another blow prior to the 1957 season when petrol rationing was introduced in the wake of the Suez crisis. Yet another London track, Wembley, pulled out along with Poole, leaving only twelve teams in the top two divisions, which were forced to amalgamate into just one National League. For the first time, all three of East Anglia's competing teams – Norwich, Rayleigh and Ipswich – were

Norwich's Ove Fundin and Harry Edwards lead Ipswich's Alby Golden in a shot from the match held on 17 August 1957.

in the same league. As well as this league, the Southern Area League, the successor to the old Metropolitan League, continued to run with four teams.

Norwich turned in their best performance for some time as the World Champion, Ove Fundin, recorded an outstanding performance, averaging 13.67 for the season, while Aub Lawson returned to the sort of form he had shown in the immediate post-war years, with an average of 12.4. Solid support was, as usual, given by Phil Clarke and Billy Bales and the team finished runners-up in the Britannia Shield and fourth in the league. After the first leg of the Britannia Shield final, it looked as though Norwich were certain to become champions as they held Belle Vue to a 48-48 draw in Manchester. However, Belle Vue pulled out all the stops in the return leg and defeated Norwich at the Firs by 50 points to 46 to take the title.

Both Fundin and Lawson did outstandingly well in the World Championship, though it was not to be two titles running for Fundin, as he just lost out in a run-off with Barry Briggs for first place. Lawson also lost out in a run-off, this time to Peter Craven for third place. So Norwich had finished up the season with the numbers two and four in the world.

Fundin also challenged Peter Craven for the British Match Race Championship – the Golden Helmet. The rules of the competition had had to be specially altered to allow him to ride, as until then foreigners had not been allowed to take part. It was not a fairy tale ending, as Craven defeated Fundin 2-1.

For Norwich, 1958 turned out to be their best season so far in speedway's top flight, as they finished runners-up to the all-conquering Wimbledon Dons. Once again their assault on the championship was spearheaded by Ove Fundin and Aub Lawson, who was now enjoying a real

Indian summer, as he finished third in the World Championship, his highest placing ever. This time he beat Peter Craven in the run-off, streaking off from the gate and finishing alone as both Craven and Ken McKinlay, who was also in the run-off, fell. His prize for coming third was £100. Ove Fundin once again finished runner-up to Barry Briggs. By way of consolation, Fundin did manage to at last defeat Peter Craven to pick up the Golden Helmet, only to lose it later in the season to Brian Crutcher. Needless to say, Phil Clarke and Billy Bales provided the necessary support as did the newcomer to the team, Johnnie Chamberlain. Bales was chosen to ride for England against Sweden at Norwich and scored 11 points.

Following the withdrawal of Rayleigh and Ipswich, Norwich once again became East Anglia's only representative in the National League but they did not have quite as good a season as the previous one, finishing fourth. Inevitably, Ove Fundin and Aub Lawson spearheaded Norwich's attack with solid support coming from Billy Bales, Cyril Roger, Phil Clarke, Reg Trott, Johnnie Chamberlain, Harry Edwards and new signing from Ipswich, Peter Moore.

In the World Championship, Ove Fundin yet again finished runner-up, this time to Ronnie Moore and yet again, Aub Lawson was involved in a run-off for third place, this time finishing fifth overall behind Briggs and Olle Nygren. Cyril Roger also qualified for the final, coming last with no points. Both Lawson and Moore were chosen for Australasia in all six Test matches, with Chamberlain being chosen for one, while Reg Trott was chosen once for England.

Norwich faced the new era of the swinging sixties without the familiar bespectacled face of Phil Clarke, who had decided to call it a day at the end of the 1959 season. Clarke had first ridden for the Stars in 1947 and had remained ever since, being one of the few riders in the history of the sport to spend his whole career exclusively with one club. By the time he had finished he had ridden in 309 matches for the club and scored 2,162 points, both club records which were never beaten and which amounted to a career record of 6.99 points per match.

Ove Fundin advertises Norwich speedway from the back of a Truman's cart.

The rest of the team was little changed, although a new name was added to the team sheet during the season, a young seventeen-year-old rider by the name of Terry Betts, who was destined to become one of the finest riders ever produced by East Anglia. Paddy Mills attempted a comeback and raced Betts for a place in the team, but he had been out of the saddle too long and decided to give up the attempt.

Once again, Norwich had a fairly average year with the main bulk of the scoring falling to Fundin, who averaged an incredible 16 points for the year, and Lawson, ably backed by Bales, Trott and Chamberlain. Terry Betts rode in four matches scoring no points! The Stars finished fifth in the League, but did reach the final of the National Trophy, which they lost to the unstoppable Wimbledon 115-101 on aggregate.

There is no doubt, however, that 1960 was once again Ove Fundin's year. He began the season by taking the Match Race title away from Crutcher and successfully defending it against Craven and McKinlay, finally losing it by default to Craven at the end of the season when he had to return home to Sweden after drawing the first two legs. He finished the season by becoming World Champion again, having finished runner-up for the previous three years. This time he made no mistake and took the title after a three-way run-off with Ronnie Moore and Peter Craven.

The Norwich crowd witnessed a tragic event in July when Belle Vue's Derek 'Tink' Maynard was killed during a National Trophy match and his team-mate Maurice Payling was seriously injured.

Norwich began the 1961 season without Aub Lawson for the first time since he had arrived in 1953. He had intended to return from his home in Australia for the start of the new season,

Left: *Phil Clarke only ever rode for Norwich, making more appearances and scoring more points than anyone else in the club's history.* Right: *Aub Lawson at full throttle.*

but his wife had become seriously ill and Lawson decided to stay with her. He never rode in England again. There is no doubt that Lawson, an automatic choice for Australia and later Australasia, was one of the greatest riders of all time. He had one of the longest careers of any top rider. In all he qualified for the World Championship final twelve times and finished third once, fourth twice and fifth once.

He was by inclination a leg trailer, but realised soon after the war that if he wanted to reach the very top flight he would have to convert to foot forward. Nevertheless, he continued to be a spectacular rider, and anyone who ever saw him will never forget his all action style, scarf streaming out behind him, as he took on and beat the best in the world. His decision to stay at home was a sad loss to Norwich, who were unable to find a suitable replacement in time for the new season. As a consequence, Norwich dropped down the table to finish in seventh place, with Fundin the only rider in the top twenty of the league averages, with 12.47. The next best rider was Johnnie Chamberlain at number thirty with an average of 6.71.

Fundin was more or less carrying the team at this period and once again he had an outstanding year in 1961, winning the World Championship for the third time, and capturing the Match Race Championship from old rival Peter Craven.

New Cross, who had returned to the National League in 1960, dropped out again at the end of the 1961 season and two of their riders, Eric Williams and Jimmy Gooch, moved to Norwich. Other than that the 1962 team remained much the same as the previous season, although ex-Norfolk cycle speedway champion, Trevor Hedge, was pencilled in as reserve. The Stars had a most unfortunate start to the season as on 31 March, just ten minutes before the meeting was due to take place, snow fell and the meeting had to be cancelled.

Injuries to Ove Fundin and Billy Bales meant that Norwich never found themselves in any position to challenge for league honours. Olle Nygren and Gote Nordin stood in for Fundin. Gooch proved to be a useful asset, but Williams couldn't settle down and retired before the end of the season. However, the revelation of the season was the young Terry Betts. Betts had been with Norwich for two seasons and although he had shown much promise he had not yet realised his potential. All that was to change on 14 July 1962. On a night that Fundin was to score a mere 4 points against Belle Vue, Betts weighed in with a 15-point maximum, including two victories over Peter Craven. From then on Betts could do no wrong and finished the season with 144 points, second only to Fundin, but Betts could not carry the team on his own and the Stars finished fifth out of seven.

In spite of his injury, Fundin had another good year, winning the Internationale for the second year running and beating Bjorn Knutsson for the Golden Helmet at the start of the season and retaining it for the rest of the year. He also finished third in the World Championship, his worst position since 1955!

Gordon Parkins had been so impressed with Olle Nygren in the five matches in which he had stood in for Fundin that he decided to sign him up permanently in time for the 1963 season. Unfortunately, Parkins ran foul of the Speedway Riders' Association (SRA), who would only allow a maximum of one foreigner per team. This left Norwich with Fundin, Betts, Debbage, Trott, Gooch, Hedge and the injured Billy Bales. Parkins felt this team was just too weak and, with no top British riders left to sign, he considered withdrawing from the league. With Ipswich having packed it in, the league was now down to seven teams. If Norwich withdrew as well, the National League would not be viable, so the Control Board called a crisis meeting between the Norwich management, the SRA and the other National League promoters to try and resolve the situation. In the end the crisis was averted and Norwich were allowed to sign Nygren.

Nygren's arrival breathed a new lease of life into the Stars, who had their best ever season, finishing as runners-up to Belle Vue in the League and winning the National Trophy, beating Belle Vue in the final. Ove Fundin once again became World Champion, which meant that from 1956 he had finished first, second, second, second, first, first, third and first. No one else had ever come anywhere near achieving this sort of consistency in the sport's toughest event.

As the 1964 season got underway Norwich were once again the only league team operating in East Anglia, but all was not well at the Firs. Terry Betts had been suspended for nine months and had had his licence withdrawn at the end of the 1963 season for non-attendance at an official meeting. At the start of the season he was allocated to Swindon, but he refused to ride there as he did not feel he was getting a fair crack of the whip from the speedway authorities. Tommy Price offered him a slot at his club, West Ham, and persuaded Betts to send a letter of apology to the Control Board. However, Betts decided in the end that he did not want to ride for West Ham and in fact was not prepared to ride at all and so, at the tender age of twenty-one, he retired from competitive speedway. George Major was offered a team place at Norwich but he decided it was too far to travel from his Hampshire home and Hungarian exile, Sandor Levai, was brought in.

Fundin and Nygren continued to dominate proceedings at the Firs as well as on many away tracks. Levai got better as the season went on and Trevor Hedge continued to show a marked

Left: *A young Terry Betts in action for Norwich.* Right: *The unmistakable style of Olle Nygren. Nygren began his riding career in 1947 and continued until the 1970s. He qualified for six World Finals, finishing third once and fourth twice.*

Left: *Derek Strutt was a good solid second string for Norwich from 1957 to 1962.* Right: *Reg Trott, captain of Norwich in their final year.*

improvement. Norwich finished the season in third place, but however good or bad the season had been became irrelevant as the management of the Firs Stadium announced that it was closing its doors forever and the site was to be sold off for redevelopment for the sum of £75,000. The riders had known for some time that this could be the Stars' last season. As skipper Reg Trott said after the final announcement was made: 'It has not been pleasant riding at Norwich with the axe always ready to fall. A thing like that changes the atmosphere of the place.'

It still seemed scarcely credible to the supporters that anything like this could happen. Gates were still healthy and amongst the best in the country, the team was doing well and the carefree clubroom atmosphere was unique in speedway. As far as they were concerned this sort of thing only happened to other tracks; Ipswich had come and gone, Rayleigh had come and gone, Yarmouth had come and gone, but not Norwich! Hadn't Norwich survived speedway's lean years of the late 1950s? And yet it was true. The Firs Stadium, which had been the centre of speedway in East Anglia since 1930, was to close. Crowds up to 25,000 strong had thrilled to the exploits of the likes of Grosskreutz, Wise, Spencer, Mills, Leverenz, Clarke, Bales, Fundin, Lawson and Nygren, but now it was all over and the Firs was to become a housing estate. Thirty-five years of history gone in a moment.

The last meeting held at Norwich was on 31 October. It was the Supporters' Trophy, which was run on a handicap basis and won by Tich Read. There was a special 'Old Stars' race between Jack Freeman, Phil Clarke, Wilf Jay and Lennie Read. The biggest disappointment of

Norwich's last team. From left to right: Billy Bales, Olle Nygren, Sandor Levai, Ove Fundin, Reg Trott (captain, on bike), John Debbage, Trevor Hedge, Tich Read.

the night was the fact that Ove Fundin, the greatest of them all, was unable to be there due to prior commitments – the meeting had originally been arranged for 14 October but had been rained off.

Shortly after this last meeting rumours flew around that Norwich speedway had been saved and that Maurice Littlechild and Jack Thompson had found a twelve-acre site at Horsford: news came through that trials had even been held. But in the end it was not to be and Norwich was never again to hear the roar of competitive league speedway.

Speedway did, however, return very briefly to Norwich at the end of 1976, when Cyril Crane staged a full-scale twenty-heat meeting at Hevingham in December. Crane and his partner, Violet Littlechild, owned the 33-acre site on which there was a 350-yard track, with banking and terracing for 15,000 spectators under construction. Despite the frosty conditions, 2,000 fans turned out to see the Norwich Supporters' Trophy. Most of the riders involved were juniors, only Cyril's nephew David was a name anyone had heard of, and even he hadn't ridden competitively for five years. The idea of the meeting was to demonstrate to the council what speedway was all about and to get them to agree to the holding of up to two dozen meetings in 1977, so that Norwich could enter the National League. The winner of the Trophy was fourteen-year-old Peterborough mascot and grass track junior, Andrew Buck.

Not everyone was happy about the staging of this meeting. Ipswich promoter John Berry, in particular, was incensed and called for the strongest possible disciplinary measures to be taken against the promoters of the meeting. His view was that an unlicensed meeting like this would give the sport a bad image and would affect others when applying for planning permission. In the end the attempt to bring speedway back to Norwich failed as Crane was unable to get the required planning permission.

Two
Yarmouth

Cashing in on the fact that Yarmouth had a speedway team, the enterprising Yarmouth Town Council advertised holidays in the Speedway Gazette, *as can be seen on this page taken from the 10 July 1948 issue.*

Yarmouth applied to join the Third Division in 1948. The new track, 350 yards in length, was at Yarmouth Stadium on Caister Road and could accommodate 10,000 spectators. Yarmouth in fact had very close ties with Norwich, with Dick Wise being promoter at both tracks, and was to all intents and purposes a training ground for them. As Wise said, if Yarmouth were going to operate it was better they did so in co-operation with Norwich rather than in opposition.

As the season started, team colours of black and amber were chosen, but the team name was to be left to a vote by local supporters. The team colours were later changed to red and black and the nickname 'Bloaters' chosen.

A pre-season announcement of riders included Roy Duke, Paddy Hammond and Bluey Thorpe from Norwich along with Ted Rawlinson, Bert Rawlinson, Les Mullins, who had been trained on Army tracks in Egypt, and the seventeen-year-old cycle speedway star, Billy Bales. By the time the season started others had been brought into the team, including Reg Craven, Bill Carruthers, Sid Hipperson and Bill Williams. The Egyptian-trained Mullins never took his place in the team, deciding he would rather become a mechanic than a rider. He eventually went on to become Ove Fundin's mechanic.

The Rawlinsons were to play a big part in the launching of Yarmouth as Ted Rawlinson won the very first race of the very first meeting, the East Coast Trophy, while Bert Rawlinson won the trophy itself. Bert Rawlinson also top scored in Yarmouth's first competitive match, a 28-52 defeat away to Hull. The first home match was also lost, this time by 38-66 to Poole in the second qualifying round of the National Trophy. There was one bright spot in this latter defeat, however, and that was the showing of Billy Bales who, in his first ever meeting, scored 10 points. Even as early as this first season, Bales showed the promise which was to bring him into the full England Test team and make him a

Yarmouth's first team. From left to right: Reg Morgan, Max Pearce, Dick Wise (manager), Roy Duke, Paddy Hammond, Bill Carruthers, Sid Hipperson, Billy Bales, Bert Rawlinson, Ted Rawlinson.

A young Billy Bales. He became a top rider with Yarmouth and Norwich from the opening of Yarmouth in 1948 to the closure of Norwich in 1964.

World Championship finalist. By the end of the season he had become the idol of the Yarmouth crowd. Dick Wise considered promoting him to the Norwich team, but decided against it. 'I just can't do it,' he said, 'they [the Yarmouth supporters] would tear me apart.'

Tragedy struck Yarmouth twice during their inaugural season. First of all, on 26 May, on the first bend of his first race in the match at Poole, Reg Craven crashed in a three-man pile-up and was taken to hospital with a fractured skull. He later died of his injuries. Secondly, after winning his first ever race as reserve for Yarmouth, Australian Max Pearce grazed the safety fence in a second-half scratch event and was flung off with such force that he also suffered a fractured skull and died later in hospital. Pearce's death was unusual as it happened at Yarmouth's thirteenth meeting on 13 July. Pearce's average at the time was 1.3!

It was unfortunate for Yarmouth that they began operations just as a pay dispute hit the Third Division, which resulted in unsettling effects for everyone concerned. The old system of grading riders for pay purposes had been replaced by a system of differentials based on which division you were riding in. Third Division riders were given 15 shillings a start and 15 shillings a point. The Riders' Association wanted this increased to £1 a start and £1 a point. This was turned down by the promoters, who claimed that this would cost an extra £20 per meeting and that new tracks would not be able to bear the burden. Yarmouth in particular was felt to be at risk if this new pay deal went through as it was reckoned that meetings needed to attract crowds of between 4,500 and 5,000 to break even. Yarmouth's opening fixture had attracted just 2,900.

YARMOUTH SPEEDWAY RIDER KILLED

Max Pearce, 23-year-old Yarmouth speedway rider, died in Yarmouth Hospital this morning from injuries suffered in an accident at the Caister Road Stadium last night.

Pearce, who had recorded his first heat win since joining Yarmouth in the Div. III. match with Coventry, was competing in the last but one of the second-half scratch races.

He was lying fourth after a bad start and was trying to make up ground on the straight. His machine wobbled, struck the safety fence and appeared to drag Pearce across the track. He was taken to hospital immediately.

Pearce, who had only been in this country a few weeks, came from Melbourne. He signed for Norwich soon after his arrival and was transferred to Yarmouth.

MAX PEARCE

SECOND FATALITY

He is the second member of the Yarmouth team to be fatally injured this season. Early in the season Reg Craven died in hospital after an accident at Poole.

Yesterday was July 13th—and it was the 13th speedway meeting of the season at Yarmouth.

A newspaper cutting reporting the fatal accident to Max Pearce on 13 July 1948.

The riders, on the other hand, complained that the average earnings of £12 per week for second strings were not enough to live on, keep machines in trim and pay for the winter months when they were not earning anything. The dispute rumbled on for some months, with the riders at one time threatening strike action. (Incidentally the decision to strike was made at a Riders' Association meeting held on 23 May 1948 at which the Association also called for eye-sight test for stewards and an end to loudspeaker slanging matches between rival team managers and promoters!) The dispute eventually ended on 9 July when the promoters and riders accepted a recommendation from the Standing Joint Committee, made up of representatives from the Association and the promoters, that Division Three riders should be paid £1 a start.

As the season went on crowds increased at Yarmouth until they were well over the break even level, averaging nearly 8,000 by the end, with the record crowd being just under 9,000. The team itself, however, did not fare so well, finishing one from bottom of the league. The top three riders were Sid Hipperson, Billy Bales and Reg Morgan and, although Hipperson had had a fair amount of experience at Norwich, Bales and Morgan were complete novices, so future prospects were looking more hopeful.

The 1949 season started well for Yarmouth on the track as they raced to four away victories at Rayleigh, Halifax, Leicester and Exeter and it became clear that the league title rested between them and Hanley (Stoke). With everything seemingly dependent on the outcome of the encounter between the two sides at Hanley on 15 October, a capacity crowd (with 20,000 people locked outside) saw a last heat 5-1 by Billy Bales and Fred Brand give Yarmouth victory by 44 points to 39. With this defeat it meant that Hanley would have to win their last two matches by large margins to snatch victory away from Yarmouth. Unfortunately for the Bloaters, a win over Hastings by 56 points to 28 and a final victory of the season over Liverpool by 58 to 24, meant that Hanley did just that, winning the league title by the slenderest of margins on points average by just 0.005 of a point! Yarmouth also lost to Hanley in the final of the Third Division round of the National Trophy by 113 points to 101.

Yarmouth's chief consolation was to see Billy Bales top the Third Division rankings for the year after scoring 473 points at an average of 10.06. Billy was still only nineteen and after one match against Rayleigh (in which he top scored), he went to the clubhouse for a drink. The attendant did not recognise him and refused him admission on the grounds that youngsters were not allowed on licensed premises! Yarmouth's other leading junior, Reg Morgan, joined him in the top ten. The whole team rode well that year, with Tip Mills, Bill Carruthers, Sid Hipperson, Johnnie White, Bert Rawlinson, Fred Brand and Stan Page all making it an excellent season for the Bloaters in only their second season in speedway and one which saw them, along with Hanley, promoted to Division Two.

Left: *Reg Morgan rode for Yarmouth throughout their first spell from 1948 to 1953.* Right: *The front cover of the Yarmouth versus Halifax programme for 2 August 1949.*

Left: *The front cover of the Yarmouth versus Poole programme for 22 September 1953, showing the Caister Road Stadium.* Right: *The bespectacled Bill Carruthers, who rode for Yarmouth from 1948 to 1950 and was captain for a brief spell in his last year.*

Although the team had performed well in the league, the management were still finding it hard going financially. They reckoned they needed crowds of 7,000 to break even and they approached local MPs to see if they could lobby for the reduction of the iniquitous Entertainment Tax. However, the Treasury were still deaf to speedway's and Yarmouth's pleadings.

In readiness for the team's promotion to Division Two, the track was relaid over the close season and was converted from cinders to shale. Unfortunately for Yarmouth, Billy Bales was called up for National Service and only managed three matches in 1950. Without Bales, the Bloaters had no chance in the higher division. They started the season by losing their first seven matches, all away from home, and, although they showed better form at home, they were never in with a chance, finishing the season in twelfth place out of fifteen. They lost every single one of their away matches, but won twelve out of fourteen at home. Top man was Fred Brand, who scored 187 points in 28 matches. Reg Morgan continued to show good form, but had never made the same sort of progress as Billy Bales. Two new Australian riders joined the team, Bill Maddern and Wally Higgs. Unfortunately, after just 16 matches, Higgs broke his leg at Walthamstow and never rode in this country again, while Maddern was not very impressive.

Bill Carruthers, who, like Phil Clarke, rode in spectacles, had been Bales's riding partner and became Yarmouth's captain in 1950. Unfortunately, after 20 matches, he broke his leg and retired from the sport. Because of this accident to Carruthers, the other riders felt there was a jinx on the captaincy and they all refused to take on the job so that Yarmouth finished the season without one.

With the better class of racing now on offer, crowds increased at the Caister Road Stadium, but new manager, Ernie Wedon, realised that he would have to strengthen his team for the 1951 season if those crowds were not to drop off due to lack of success. However, the position turned out to be much the same as the previous year, winning all but one at home and losing every match away from home to finish the league just below halfway in eleventh position. The best thing to come out of the season was the form of Fred Brand, who increased his average from 6.68 to 9.4. Bob Baker, a newcomer to the team, was also very impressive, particularly at Caister Road, and averaged 8.73 for the season. Unfortunately, there was little support for the top two. Reg Morgan had his worst year so far, as did Sid Hipperson. Vic Ridgeon proved to be a very promising junior but was in need of more experience on away tracks.

In 1951, Yarmouth had the honour of staging the first Test match ever to be held on Norfolk soil, when Britain took on a team labelled Overseas. This was a series for Second Division riders, which Britain lost 3-2, although they won the match at Yarmouth, thanks to some sterling performances by local riders. Fred Brand top scored with 17 points, Bob Baker got 14 and Phil Clarke 12 while for the Overseas side Bob Leverenz weighed in with 15 and Alec Hunter 8. Altogether, Bob Leverenz appeared in four out of the five matches, scoring a total of 52 points. Phil Clarke scored 30 from three.

The 1952 season was the same story for the third year running at the 'Bloater Pond', with Yarmouth winning all but two of their home matches, but failing to pick up a single point away. Their home form was so impressive that they even managed to beat the runaway league champions, Poole, by 58-26, but it was obvious that most of the riders had become one-track specialists, especially Reg Morgan, Vic Ridgeon, Tip Mills and Stan Page. Only Fred Brand and Bob Baker were able to mix it with the opposition on their own tracks with any degree of success, finishing the season with averages of 9.5 and 9.3 respectively. Two newcomers did show promise as Terry Courtnell averaged 6.1 and the pint-sized Australian, Johnnie Chamberlain, said to be the smallest rider ever to ride in speedway, arrived with a 4.5 average. In the end, Yarmouth finished the season in a disappointing ninth place.

The Yarmouth Test match that year saw the final humiliation of the Overseas team as Britain completed a 5-0 whitewash by a score of 80 points to 28; Fred Brand and Bob Baker both scoring 15 points. Johnnie Chamberlain was the only Overseas rider to put up any sort of opposition, scoring 9 points.

While affairs were looking bad for Norwich in 1953, things were looking decidedly up at Great Yarmouth. For the first time since joining Division Two, the Bloaters managed to win an away match. In fact, they got so carried away that they managed to win three. The reason for this upturn in their fortunes was the continued improvement of Johnnie Chamberlain and the introduction of new riders Reg Reeves and Ronnie Genz to the team to complement the established stars, Fred Brand and Bob Baker. Brand was again

Left: *Fred Brand is Yarmouth's leading points scorer of all time with a total of 1,308.* Right: *Johnnie Chamberlain, the only Yarmouth rider to race in a full Test match.*

Yarmouth's top rider with an average of 9.7, but he was closely followed by Chamberlain on 8.2 and Reeves on 7.8.

Chamberlain's improvement was so remarkable that he even forced his way in to the full Australian Test side for the match at Norwich where he scored three points from the reserve position. Incidentally, Billy Bales and Aub Lawson both scored 13 points for their respective sides in that Test match, which was won by Australia 62 points to 46.

Unfortunately for Yarmouth and Australia, Chamberlain was injured at Poole in June, shortly after the Test match, and was unable to ride again. Instead of finishing third, Yarmouth may well have won the League if he had ridden all season.

In the Second Division's own Test series, Britain versus Overseas, no less than four Yarmouth riders rode for Britain in the Yarmouth Test: Reg Reeves, who top scored with 14 points, Ronnie Genz, Terry Courtnell and Roy Bowers. As well as these four, Fred Brand had appeared in the Coventry Test and Chamberlain in the first Test at Liverpool. Olle Nygren scored 15 points in the Yarmouth Test for Overseas. This was the only one of the series which Britain lost.

There was a major tragedy for East Anglia when it was announced that one of the 1953 teams not taking part in the 1954 season was Yarmouth. Yarmouth had never wanted to start the season early as, being a seaside town, the management felt it was best to wait until the holiday crowds arrived before opening up. Early matches were an economic disaster for the club as gates were always very poor. For 1954 they applied to the Control Board for permission to start the season late and to miss the early season Northern Shield competition, preferring to wait until the Second Division proper started, but this was refused. Consequently, the Bloaters withdrew from the League altogether and their licence was taken away. Fred Brand graduated to the First Division and joined Norwich, Johnnie Chamberlain moved to Ipswich while the others spread out far and wide over the rest of the country.

However, there was good news in 1957 as the Caister Road Stadium once more echoed to the sound of speedway bikes. A crowd of 5,000 witnessed the opening meeting in which Ove Fundin defeated Peter Craven for the East Anglia Trophy. Yarmouth put on a short season of challenge matches, with a team calling itself East Anglia taking on all-comers. The team consisted of different guest riders booked to appear each week and included Barry Briggs and Peter Moore as well as giving a chance to junior riders with a view to possibly competing in the Southern Area League in 1958. In the end, Yarmouth decided not to enter the Southern Area League (SAL) after all, but continued to run a series of challenge matches in 1958 with the likes of Fundin, Lawson, Briggs and Ronnie Moore all wearing the colours of 'East Anglia'.

Action from a Yarmouth versus Norwich match, with Fred Pawson of Norwich riding round the outside of Yarmouth's Bob Baker and Ronnie Genz.

Yarmouth finally entered a team in the Southern Area League in 1959, finishing runners-up with a team that included Al Sparrey, Ivor Brown, Johnny Fitzpatrick, John Debbage and Dave Hankins. Hankins also won the Silver Sash after Gooddy had relinquished the title in July. In addition, Hankins took the SAL Individual Riders' Championship at Ipswich, sweeping through the field with a maximum. Ivor Brown was third.

The 1960 season saw the long awaited revival in the sport's fortunes as the Provincial League was born. With a crowd of over 80,000 packing the Empire Stadium for the 1959 World Championship Final and attendances reportedly up during the year at most tracks, new promoters decided to take the plunge and speedway welcomed the return of familiar names such as Bristol, Sheffield, Liverpool, Cradley Heath, Stoke, Edinburgh and Bradford to take part in the newly formed Provincial League. Also applying to join the Provincial League were Yarmouth and the re-formed Rayleigh Rockets under their new promoters, Wally Mawdsley and Pete Lansdale. There were also two new entries in the National League, London track New Cross and Ipswich, who had taken over the Poole team on the latter's move into the Provincial League. In all there were now twenty major

Left: *Johnny Fitzpatrick, seen here in Ipswich colours, was a leading member of the Yarmouth Provincial League team.* Right: *John Debbage rode for Yarmouth from 1959 to 1960. He moved on to Norwich in 1961 and stayed until they closed in 1964.*

*Programme cover for the opening meeting of
1961, Yarmouth's last ever season.*

league teams, ten in the National League and ten in the Provincial League. Four of these
were based in East Anglia.

Yarmouth's attempt at league honours was not successful with the team finishing in
seventh place. Ivor Brown was top man just ahead of evergreen Geoff Pymar, who had
once again returned to his roots in East Anglia. Johnny Fitzpatrick, Ron Bagley, Ken Last
and John Debbage made up the rest of the team.

Towards the end of the their short season, Yarmouth ran into some very bad weather
and the crowds were poor. The management decided against running a team in the
following year's Provincial League and, instead, opted to return to running challenge
matches on an open licence.

Yarmouth took part in a competition called the East Anglian League, which consisted
of Norwich 'B', Ipswich 'B', Rayleigh and themselves. Although Ivor Brown was now a
Cradley rider, he continued to ride for Yarmouth in this league, scoring 24 points in three
matches. Brown, in fact, finished the season by far and away the top scorer in the
Provincial League, 72 points ahead of his nearest rival, Harry Bastable (also of Cradley),
and 111 points in front of next man, Ken Adams.

Yarmouth's last meeting of the season was the King's of Oxford Trophy, held on 8 August
1961 and won by the Lemon Drop Kid, Pete Jarman. Speedway racing was never to be seen
in the town again.

Three
Rayleigh

Programme cover from 1949, Rayleigh's first full league season.

In the south of the region, another new team came into being in 1948 as, on the 4 June, ex-bomber pilot Frank Arnold was given permission by the Control Board to open up a 385-yard track at Rayleigh in Essex. For 1948, Arnold ran a series of open meetings trying to build up a team with which he could enter Division Three in 1949. Rayleigh's opening fixture, in front of a crowd of 12,000, was against Leicester and resulted in a 51-32 win for the home side. Captain Ron Howes, brought in from Wimbledon, scored 11 and Bruce Abernethy, on loan from Wembley, got 9. Special trains were laid on to bring spectators to Rayleigh Weir from Enfield Town, Alexandra Palace and Chingford for 3s 3d return.

Arnold said he was prepared to spend up to £2,000 on transfer fees to get the team ready for the 1949 Division Three campaign and, although he was unable to secure the permanent transfer of his number one target, Bruce Abernethy, he did manage to recruit a couple of seasoned performers in Percy Brine from Fleetwood and Billy Newell from Plymouth. He also trained a number of youngsters up to Division Three standard, including Jim Gregory and Vic Gooden.

Rayleigh's first full season in league racing was to prove something of a disappointment. Not many of the team Frank Arnold had put together to race challenge matches the previous year stayed and he was left with a team consisting mainly of novices and juniors. Although many of these showed promise – such as Pat Clarke, Jack Unstead, Jim Gregory and Les McGillivray – they weren't yet ready to be the mainstay of a league team. Clarke was probably the pick of the juniors, having been a graduate of the 'Aussie' Powell school. He scored a maximum after just a month in the team and finished the season as captain. He had a narrow escape early in the season when he cannoned off the inner edge while racing at Leicester and ran into Roy Duke. Clarke's bike jumped the fence and both men had to be carried off. Fortunately, Clarke only suffered minor injuries, while Duke had to be taken to hospital suffering from a broken leg. Jack Unstead was another Powell discovery who scored a maximum in only his second match, while Jim Gregory had been in the 1948 experimental line-up on loan from Wembley. He was transferred during the close season for £50 and finished the season with an average of 5.87. Les McGillivray came into the side later in the season but finished top of the averages with 6.47. The more experienced Ron Howes was disappointing and managed only 188 points from 47 matches.

Rayleigh finished the season one from bottom and were the only team to fail to win a single away match. They also went out in the first round of the National Trophy qualifying competition to Yarmouth.

At one time during the 1949/50 close season it looked as though Rayleigh might fold. However, the team was taken over by a former West Ham rider and now manager, Arthur Atkinson, and his wife. Once again many of the previous year's team had departed and Rayleigh were left with Jack Unstead, Ron Howes and Vic Gooden. Les McGillivray was still on the books, but was called up into the forces. Fortunately, all three – Unstead, Howes and Gooden – improved on their 1949 performances, but it was newcomer Gerald Jackson who set the Rayleigh crowd alight as, in only his third match, he scored a maximum and went on to top the team's averages at the end of the season. Jackson was the son of former Wembley rider, Jack Jackson, and had been spotted by West Ham star

 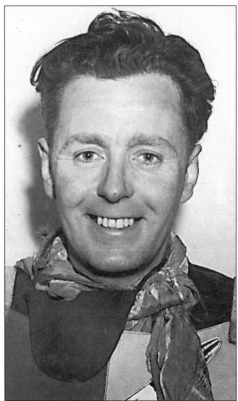

Left: *Bruce Abernethy, a New Zealander, was loaned to Rayleigh for the 1948 season from his parent club, Wembley.* Right: *Ron Howes made 163 official appearances for Rayleigh between 1949 and 1954.*

Aub Lawson whilst taking part in a Sunday meeting at California in Berkshire. After a few outings at Custom House, Jackson was transferred by Arthur Atkinson to his Rayleigh outfit: at this time Rayleigh had the same sort of relationship with West Ham as Yarmouth did with Norwich. Other new riders brought into the team included Frank Bettis, another West Ham rider, Charles Mugford and Tom O'Connor. Although finishing just one place above the cellar position, there was a great deal of optimism about the future as the juniors continued to improve and the team began to gel together.

Sure enough, the following season, Rayleigh at last began to show the sort of form that had been promised but not delivered the year before. From next to bottom in 1950, the Rockets rose to fourth place in 1951. Gerald Jackson continued to go from strength to strength and recorded an 8 point average. Jack Unstead also had a good season, finishing third in the Division Three Riders' Championship. New signing Maurice Dunn, a New Zealander making his first appearance in this country, proved to be a great asset and finished up with a 7.74 average. Another newcomer from New Zealand, Jules Benson, did not show quite the same aptitude, but nevertheless showed distinct promise. Les McGillivray managed to put in 16 performances in between his National Service duties and, along with Tom O'Connor, gave the team a very powerful second string middle order. As performances improved so did the crowds, and the future for Rayleigh now looked very bright.

The Third Division held three series of Test matches, against Sweden, New Zealand and USA. Two of the five Tests against New Zealand were held at Ipswich and Rayleigh. Maurice Dunn rode in all five, scoring 32 points, while Tom O'Connor, Les McGillivray, Jack Unstead, Gerald Jackson and Jules Benson rode in the match at Rayleigh, which England won by 70 points to 38, although they lost the series 3-2. Jack Unstead also appeared in all three Test matches against Sweden, while Gerald Jackson rode twice against America.

A reorganisation of the leagues took place in 1952, with the Third Division being renamed the Southern League in an attempt to cut down on transport costs. Entertainment Tax was still taking its toll of speedway, having risen to 60% in August 1951, and about half the clubs finished the year in the red. Reduced pay scales were introduced with Division One riders earning 30 shillings a start, 40 shillings a point, Division Two riders were paid 20 shillings a start, 26 shillings a point and Southern League riders earning 20 shillings a start and 20 shillings a point.

Things were much healthier for East Anglia in the new Southern League as Rayleigh romped away with the title. The season started off inauspiciously with the departure of Maurice Dunn back to his parent track Harringay, but in his place Peter Clark was

Left: Maury Dunn proved a great asset to Rayleigh in his one season with them in 1951 before he moved on to First Division Harringay. He was later killed in a motor boat accident. Right: Programme cover for the Southern League match against Ipswich on 28 June 1952, showing an aerial view of the Weir Stadium.

recruited. Clark settled in quickly and by the end of the season was being hailed 'Discovery of the Year'. Another outstanding recruit was Maury McDermott from Harringay. Les McGillivray also returned from National Service to boost the team in the latter half of the season. In the end Rayleigh ran away with the league title, a clear ten points in front of runners-up Cardiff. Gerald Jackson topped the averages with 8.9, followed closely by Jack Unstead on 8.8. In the Southern League rankings for 1952, Jack Unstead was in third place, Jackson in fourth and Peter Clark in sixth. Three riders in the top six out of a division of ten teams demonstrated, as much as the league title itself, Rayleigh's superiority.

The following year, the destination of the Southern League Championship was fought out between reigning champions, Rayleigh, and the West Country's top team, Exeter. Regrettably, however, most of the action was being fought out behind the closed doors of the Speedway Control Board rather than on the track. On 18 April, Rayleigh lost at home to Exeter by 39 points to 45. Rayleigh immediately lodged a protest that Exeter had used Jack Geran as reserve in contravention of rule number 506, which said that a reserve must not be a man who had scored 50 per cent or more in his six preceding fixtures. Rayleigh's protest was upheld and the match was expunged from the records, thus depriving Exeter of the two match points. By 28 September it became clear that the title rested between

Left: *Peter Clark, hailed 'Discovery of the Year' in 1952, stayed with the Rockets until 1955.* Right: *Gerald Jackson, Rayleigh's most prolific scorer of all time, stayed with the club from 1950 until 1956.*

The 1953 Rayleigh team. From left to right, back row: Maurice McDermott, Tom O'Connor, Alby Smith, Les McGillivray. Front row: Frank Bettis, Peter Clark, Gerald Jackson, Ron Howes.

Rayleigh and Exeter, with the Devon team needing four points from their two remaining fixtures to clinch the title. One of those matches was against Rayleigh. Unfortunately for Rayleigh, Les McGillivray had been injured two nights earlier and although the Rockets sent a full eight-man team down to the County Ground they wanted to make last-minute alterations to the published pairings. The steward was not prepared to let them do this and would only agree to another rider taking the place of the injured McGillivray. Rayleigh announced they would race under protest and immediately after the meeting, which Exeter won by 60 points to 24, they lodged an appeal with the Control Board. Exeter drew their last remaining fixture at Southampton and this put them on level points with Rayleigh, but they were declared champions by virtue of having scored more race points.

On the following Friday the Control Board upheld Rayleigh's appeal, once again expunging Exeter's victory from the record books and handing the league title to Rayleigh. It was now Exeter's turn to appeal and in December the RAC stewards ordered the Control Board to re-hear the case. The board upheld its decision but would only 'recommend' to the ACU that the result of the meeting be 'annulled'. As the 1954 season dawned it was still not clear who had won the 1953 title. In the end, the ACU did not accept the board's recommendation and the result stood, leaving Exeter as Southern League champions and Rayleigh as runners-up. They had started the 1953 campaign at a terrific pace, scoring six consecutive victories before losing to Swindon 44-40. A mid-season stutter, when they lost to St Austell and drew with Ipswich, was just enough to lose them the title. The team's top riders were once again Gerald Jackson, who had an average of 9.1, and Peter Clark with 8.7. Jack Unstead had left the Rockets to try his hand in the First Division with Bristol. Jackson and Clark were named as numbers two and three in the Southern League rankings for 1953, sandwiched between Exeter's Goog Hoskin and

Jack Geran. Les McGillivray was also returning to his best form with an average of 7.1 and Maury McDermott was improving all the time.

During 1953, Filbyterna, a touring team from Sweden, came over to this country to compete in a five match series against Southern League clubs. Their first match was against Rayleigh, to whom they lost by 32 points to 52. Top scorer for the Swedish club was a young nineteen-year-old former motocross rider from Tranas called Ove Fundin, who was making his first appearance in this country. The youngster learnt quickly and by the end of the series he had scored a total of 54 points at an average of 10.8.

With the reorganisation of the leagues in 1954, Rayleigh entered the Second Division – but they soon wished they hadn't as the season was a complete disaster. The Rockets won just four matches throughout the entire season, finishing in last place, ten points behind the next nearest team, Motherwell.

Following their dreadful season in 1954, Rayleigh pulled themselves together and managed to turn in a much more satisfying performance the following year, finishing third in the league. As a result of this, and of the good racing served up every week, crowds increased and were well above the average for the Second Division. The track had also been well prepared for the season, so much so in fact that the track record was shattered three times. Outstanding among the Rayleigh riders was New Zealander Peter Clark, who averaged 10.8 for the season. He received strong support from Rockets' favourites Les McGillivray, Gerald Jackson and Jack Unstead, now returned from Bristol. Former New Cross star, Bill Longley, attempted a comeback with Rayleigh, but could only manage 18 points from 8 matches. Peter Clark rode in five of the six Tests for Australasia.

Things continued to go well for Rayleigh in 1956 as the Rockets retained third place in the league. For most of the season any one of three teams looked as though they could win the title – Rayleigh, Swindon and Southampton. In the end it was Swindon who took the title, but not before Rayleigh had defeated them on their own track. At home the Rockets were unbeatable, racking up over 60 points no less than seven times. It was almost a relief when Swindon came along in the last match of the season to lose by only two points. At least the crowd saw a real match for a change. As far as matches with the other title contenders went there was a complete reversal of fortunes as Rayleigh defeated Southampton by 67-29 and 62-34 at home, yet lost 60-36 and 63-33 at Banister Court.

Once again it was Jack Unstead, Gerald Jackson and Les McGillivray who formed the backbone of the team. Pete Lansdale, who had been at the club for three seasons, showed much improved form as he finished with 170 points from his 22 matches and newcomer Alan Smith also proved his worth by scoring 166 points from the same number of matches. Jack Unstead had the honour of being chosen as reserve for England's first Test match against Sweden.

The Rayleigh team got themselves involved in controversy when they signed a petition denouncing the new rear tyre which had been introduced by the Control Board on 30 April. The petition went unheeded as the board made the tyre compulsory for all riders on 20 August.

By the time 1957 came around, things were not looking so good down at the Weir and at one time it looked as though Rayleigh might go out of business altogether. However, at the last minute, former rider Vic Gooden took over at Weir Stadium and not only

Les McGillivray, seen here wearing Hackney's kit, rode for Rayleigh from 1949 to 1957 and returned again in 1963.

continued to run Rayleigh Rockets in the National League, but also entered a team, Rayleigh Rovers, in the Southern Area League. As far as the Rockets went, however, it was not a happy season. Gerald Jackson had left and gone to Wimbledon and Alan Smith had also left. Their places had been taken by Ken Adams from Ipswich and, later in the season, the Swede, Birger Forsberg, who put some pep into Rayleigh's team by scoring a maximum on his first appearance. Les McGillivray and Jack Unstead yet again carried the team, but now with the problem of having to face teams like Wimbledon, Belle Vue and Norwich, they were in desperate need of at least one strong heat leader and they never found one. The Rockets unhappy season finished with them rooted firmly to the foot of the table.

The wandering Southern Rovers, a Southern Area League team without a home of its own, was given a base by Vic Gooden at Rayleigh. The team, consisting of Stan Clark, a former Ipswich rider, Brian Meredith, Leo McAuliffe, Tommy Sweetman and Vic Hall, proved too strong for the opposition and walked off with the league title. Leo McAuliffe also won the Southern Area Riders' Championship and was Silver Sash match race champion.

Disaster struck East Anglia at the end of the 1957 season when Rayleigh, who had nearly gone in to liquidation the winter before, decided it could no longer keep going and pulled the plug on operations. This meant the loss of two teams in one fell swoop as it put paid to both the Rockets and the Rovers. The National League was now down to ten teams for 1958 as Birmingham had also pulled out during the previous season. Rayleigh had intended to enter a team in the SAL, but withdrew at the last minute.

A Rayleigh Rockets car sticker.

The new Provincial League, formed in 1960 (see previous chapter on Yarmouth), was totally dominated by just three teams – Bristol, Poole and Rayleigh – with Rayleigh narrowly taking the honours by race points, having finished on the same number of match points as Poole (32) and just two ahead of Bristol. Sheffield, the next nearest team, could only manage 18.

Rayleigh's team consisted of top scorer and former 'Bloater' Reg Reeves, Eric Hockaday, Alan Smith, promoter and rider Pete Lansdale, Stan Stevens, Clive Hitch and Roy Craighead. Lansdale's fellow promoter, Wally Mawdsley, also rode in one match. Reeves finished with 252 points from 22 matches, while Eric Hockaday came third in the Provincial Riders' Championship.

Rayleigh were unable to hold onto their league title in 1961 and dropped to fifth place. This was mainly due to the fact that the Rayleigh management opened a new track at Exeter and transferred a number of the riders to their new venture, including Eric Hockaday, who then moved on to Stoke, and Pete Lansdale. Harry Edwards and Bob Thomas were brought in to boost the side but they could not make up for the loss of Lansdale and Hockaday. One bright spot was Reg Reeves winning the Provincial League Riders' Championship at Harringay, but luck played a big part in this victory as, going into their last race, Reg Reeves and Trevor Redmond were joint leaders on 12 points, having been undefeated all night. Redmond shot away from the tapes and was holding a clear lead when his chain came off on the very last bend, handing victory to Reeves.

Things were looking bad for East Anglian speedway in 1962 as Rayleigh decided not to run in the Provincial League that year and Ipswich pulled out mid-season, leaving only Norwich to carry the flag.

Rayleigh reappeared in 1963 under new promoter Gordon Cox. He named Maury McDermott, Derek Strutt, Vic Ridgeon, Harry Edwards, Terry Stone, Pat McKenzie, John Bailey and nineteen-year-old Austrian Gunther Freudlander as his team for the Provincial League. Phil Bishop was appointed team manager. It was good to have Rayleigh back, but the team failed to live up to expectations and they finished last, winning just 5 matches out of 24 and withdrawing once again from the league at the end of the season.

On 16 February 1963, the *Speedway Star* reported that the directors of Southend greyhound stadium had asked Wimbledon promoter, Ronnie Greene, if he would be interested in running National League speedway at the stadium. The plans still had to be approved by the local council, but there was talk of a team consisting of Jack Young, Ronnie Genz, Jack Biggs, Gordon McGregor, Split Waterman, Chum Taylor and a young up and coming star called Ivan Mauger. Gordon Cox was said to have received the news with mixed feelings.

Left: *Reg Reeves, seen here wearing Yarmouth's kit (for whom he rode in 1952 and 1953), spearheaded Rayleigh's Provincial League championship winning team of 1960.* Right: *Two former Rayleigh riders, Stan Clark and Maurie McDermott, tried to revive Rayleigh's fortunes in 1964 and ran a season of Open Meetings. This is the programme cover from the first meeting of the season.*

Although they had pulled out of the league, Rayleigh did open their gates for the 1964 season on an open licence. Under their new promoters, Wally Clark, Stan Clark and Maurice McDermott, Rayleigh put together a team to run a series of challenge matches and, later in the season, to take part in a revival of the old Metropolitan League with Eastbourne, Weymouth, Newpool (a combination of Newport and Poole juniors) and Ipswich with a view to getting a team together for the 1965 Provincial League campaign. There was talk at one time of Rayleigh running their meetings within the orbit of the National League and they actually arranged for the opening match of the season to be a challenge match against Norwich. However, the powers that be would not allow Fundin and Nygren to take part as the rules stated that there were to be 'no foreigners allowed' on open tracks. So Rayleigh decided to throw in their lot with the Provincial League instead, which at that time was operating unofficially following a dispute with the Control Board.

The new Rockets consisted of some old favourites: Roy Bowers, Stan Clark, Harry Edwards, Maurie McDermott, Vic Ridgeon and Sandy McGillivray. Later in the season they were joined by Ron Sharp, Mike Comber, Clive Hitch and the remarkable Tyburn Gallows, whose real name was Richard Humphreys, but who had changed it by deed poll. It was said that at one time he had been Britain's assistant hangman – whether this story was true or not, no one ever really found out.

With the formation of the British League in 1965, Rayleigh once again applied for an open licence with a view to operating in the new league in 1966. In the event, they managed two meetings before calling it a day.

Terry Stone was a Rayleigh stalwart from 1961 until their closure in 1973. He once turned up at a meeting having run out of petrol at Upminster and filling his car up with 'dope'. Always popular with supporters, Terry organised the placing of the commemorative plaque in the Sainsbury's which now occupies the site of Rayleigh Weir stadium.

The 1969 Rayleigh team. From left to right, back row: Mike Gardner, Dingle Brown, Dennis Mannion, Roger Wright, Terry Stone, Laurie Etheridge. Front row, on bike: Len Silver (promoter), Geoff Maloney (captain).

The British League proved to be a major success and by 1968 speedway was entering another boom period as nine new tracks opened and a British League Second Division was formed. The good news for East Anglia was that one of those teams was Rayleigh, who after a three year lay-off decided to give it another go, this time under the leadership of former Ipswich rider, Len Silver, at the time promoter at First Division Hackney. In the *Speedway Star* of 29 March 1968 he was quoted as saying that he was looking for a new start with Rayleigh: 'The team nickname will be new, for a start. The old name, the Rockets, is to be discarded. The Rockets had such a chequered career, says Silver, that he wants to get in with a completely new approach.' What happened to that idea? Silver got together a team consisting of skipper Graeme Smith, Alan Jackson, Geoff Maloney, Dennis Mannion, Mike Gardner, Laurie Etheridge, Terry Stone, Colin Tucker and Dingle Brown. A reasonably successful season saw them finish in fifth place.

Rayleigh had a very solid look about them in 1969 but failed to live up to their promise, although a second year in fifth place must rate as a fairly successful season. Graeme Smith was outstanding for the Rockets, scoring an average of 10.74 and representing Young Australia in all five Test matches against Young England and finishing up top scorer for the tourists. He received good support from Laurie Etheridge, Mike Gardner, Geoff Maloney, Roger Wright and Dingle Brown, all of whom scored over 7 points per match.

Rayleigh had a most inauspicious start to the 1970s, losing five riders before the 1970 season even started, while Dingle Brown was injured during the season and only took part in seven matches. Geoff Maloney was given the captaincy and this seemed to inspire him

Geoff Maloney in action at Rayleigh. Maloney rode for Rayleigh from 1968 to 1972 and was captain for the last four years.

as he came on like a house on fire. Thrilling to watch and a good team man, he finished the season top of the averages and saved Rayleigh from heading straight to the bottom of the league. Newcomer Hughie Saunders, the Channel Islander signed from Eastbourne in mid-season, gave good support as did Alan Jackson and Terry Stone, but it was clear to all that a mid-table position was the best that could be hoped for. That they finished twelfth out of seventeen was a tribute to the Rockets' fighting spirit and to Maloney's captaincy.

Rayleigh fared much better in 1971 as Hughie Saunders hit the big time. He failed to record double-figure scores in only four matches. Saunders was also called on frequently by parent track Hackney and did not let them down either. The new signing from Reading, Australian Bob Young, was an ever-present and provided a solid third heat leader backing to the top two. Alan Emmett and Nigel Rackett also weighed in with 6-point averages and the result was a surge up the table to fifth place. Saunders reached the final of the Division Two Riders' Championship where he finished third.

The Rayleigh team lived up to its full potential in 1972. Hugh Saunders left for a permanent spot with Hackney, leaving Geoff Maloney as number one man, and he took his chance so well that, before the season was over, he too was moved up to the Division One team by Len Silver. Before he left he recorded an average score of 10.34. Both Bob Young and Allen Emmett improved on their previous year's performances, while replacements for the two Hackney-bound men, Brian Foote and Trevor Barnwell, also turned in good team performances, with strong backing from Dingle Brown. The all-round team effort pushed Rayleigh up the table to fourth place and left them as favourites to take the 1973 title.

However, 1973 was the year when Rayleigh's luck finally ran out. Initially, it seemed that everything was in place for another good season. Bob Young was back for the start of the campaign as were Allen Emmett, Dingle Brown, Trevor Barnwell, Tiger Beech, Terry Stone and Pete Wigley. Allen Emmett in particular looked set for a good season as he rattled off 11 points in the opening match against Scunthorpe and the Rockets raced to a 52-26 victory. Then disaster struck as he broke his leg and was out for the rest of the season. In his place, Rayleigh brought in the veteran campaigner and old East Anglian favourite, Peter Moore, who managed to break his wrist. Fortunately, he wasn't out for long and came back to top the averages. Then Trevor Barnwell broke his wrist, his ankle and his foot all in quick succession, Dingle Brown asked for a move and Pete Wigley suffered from a chest infection. Pete Cairns and Les Ott were brought into the team and Cairns started off with the remarkable figures of 24 points from 2 meetings. However, he couldn't keep up the pace and finished with an average of just under 5. Les Ott broke his collar bone, and to top it all, Peter Moore finished the season breaking his leg. The net result of all this was that Rayleigh finished bottom of the league and Peter Moore finally

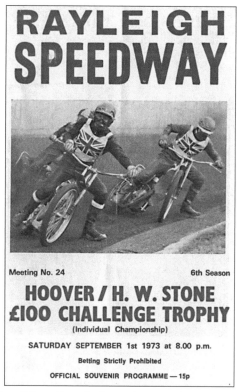

Left: *During his long career, Peter Moore rode for four different East Anglia tracks: Ipswich, Norwich, King's Lynn and Rayleigh.* Right: *Programme cover from Rayleigh's last season.*

Allen Emmett joined Rayleigh in 1970 and stayed until their closure at the end of 1973.

quit speedway in East Anglia after an on-off affair lasting almost twenty years. 'Piccolo Pete' as he was known, was born in Melbourne in 1929 and took up speedway at the age of twenty. He came to England in 1951 to ride for St Austell before joining Long Eaton in 1952 and then Wimbledon, where he blossomed into one of Australia's top riders. He was loaned to Ipswich in 1957 and 1958 and went to Norwich for a short while in 1959. He returned to Ipswich in 1960 and stayed until they folded up in 1962. In 1966 he answered King's Lynn's call for an established heat leader to start off their British League campaign. He appeared in four World Finals, his best being in 1960 when he finished fourth. He was also a regular for Australasia in Test matches during the 1950s and early '60s.

The worst news of all for Rayleigh was that in spite of good crowd figures – an average of around 5,000 – the site had been sold for redevelopment and was to become a Sainsbury's supermarket. At first it was hoped that Len Silver would be able to find a site nearby, and there was talk of moving to a track on the A130 between Carpenters Road and Canvey Island, but it never happened and the team was split up, with some going to Rye House, others to Crayford.

With the stadium being sold for redevelopment, it meant that there would never be speedway at the Weir again. Although it had had a chequered career, it had provided speedway racing on and off for twenty-five years and had produced a number of good riders in its time. Les McGillivray had ridden the most times for the team, making 216 appearances between 1948 and 1963, followed closely by Gerald Jackson with 209 and Jack Unstead with 204. Gerald Jackson had been top points scorer with 1,720 followed by Unstead with 1,614 and McGillivray with 1,604.

Four
Ipswich

Programme cover from Ipswich's first full league season in 1952.

The first hint that another East Anglian track might open came in 1948 when Ipswich applied for a licence. Unfortunately, the application was turned down by the Control Board on 13 August. There was better news two years later in 1950, however, as Arthur Franklyn, a former Belle Vue rider, together with showman D.F. Bostock and local solicitor and ex-president of the Ipswich and District Motorcycle and Car Club, R.W. Fison, formed a company with the intention of promoting speedway at a new track near Ipswich called Foxhall Heath.

The 415-yard track was tried out for the first time in October 1950 by some of the Norwich riders, with Phil Clarke recording the best time of 72.2 seconds for a four-lap clutch start. The aim was to run a series of challenge matches and junior races in 1951 with a view to forming a team ready to attain Division Three status by 1952.

Ipswich's first season saw crowds improve from an opening gate of 5,000 to an average of 9,000 over the 14 meetings and there was every confidence that Ipswich would make a success of league racing. Harold McNaughton was signed from Southampton as were Dick Shepherd, a former Walthamstow rider, Dick Laudrum and Derek Hewitt. The nucleus for the 1952 team was ready and this was to be supplemented by juniors. Junior practice was to continue throughout the winter months in an effort to find the right youngsters. Lighting was installed ready for evening racing and the Supporters' Club reported a membership of 2,000 by the end of 1951.

Walthamstow's Sid Clark became a regular at Ipswich and scored the first maximum ever recorded at Foxhall Heath, representing the Witches in a challenge match against Poole, for whom a sixteen-year-old 'wonder kid' by the name of Brian Crutcher starred. Ipswich had their own sixteen-year-old hopeful called Alby Smith who scored 7 points from 4 starts. Incidentally, the difference between the standard of Division Two and Division Three racing can be shown by the fact that the nearest anyone came to Phil Clarke's track record of 72.2 seconds was Buster Brown's 74.4, which, because it had occurred under competitive conditions, became the official track record even though it was 2.2 seconds slower.

Although Ipswich could hardly be said to have set the division alight in 1952, they did enough to show that they were here to stay. When the idea of laying a new speedway track in a wood just outside the town was mooted, many people had felt the venture was doomed to failure because of its distance from Ipswich and because the stadium itself lacked covered accommodation. However, manager Arthur Franklyn knew what he was doing as he patiently and steadily built up a team based around a few established stars and discoveries from his own winter training school. Sid Clark was appointed captain, Dick Shepherd and Harold McNaughton filled the remaining heat-leader berths, Charles Mugford from Rayleigh and Alby Smith came in as second strings while two local lads, Tich Read and Dennis Day, completed the line-up. Sid Clark proved to be the equal of any rider in the league, finishing the season with an average of 8.7, while the rest of the team formed themselves into a solid scoring outfit and, although they lost as many matches at home as they won, the scores were usually close and gave promise of better things to come. Enthusiasm was high, gates were high and everything at Ipswich looked set for a long run in league speedway.

Harold McNaughton became the first ever Ipswich rider to ride at international level when he rode in the Southern League series of representative matches against Sweden at Southampton, scoring 7 points. Sid Clark rode later in the series at Rayleigh, scoring 6 points.

Left: *Sid Clark was Ipswich's first captain and the team's first rider to score a maximum. He rode for Ipswich from 1951 to 1954.* Right: *Tich Read rode for Ipswich from 1953 to 1956 and later went on to ride for Norwich.*

Four Rayleigh riders also represented the Southern League in that match: Tom O'Connor, Jack Unstead, Gerald Jackson and Maury McDermott. Sweden's top rider in the series was a young Olle Nygren, a name which was to crop up many times in the history of East Anglian speedway.

Having expected great things from the 1953 season, Ipswich had a dreadful start and it seemed certain they would finish bottom of the league. New signings Doug Papworth, Charles Grenzel and Jim Blythe were badly injured and missed most of the season. Another new signing, Bert Edwards, was injured in his first meeting and also missed several matches. But suddenly, in mid-season, the tide turned and Ipswich stormed through to take third spot in the league, winning six and drawing one of their last eight fixtures. Sid Clark topped the scores with 185 points from 25 matches, while Bert Edwards returned to turn in an average of 7.2. Harold McNaughton averaged 5.8 and Tich Read 5.5. A promising newcomer who scored 18 points in 6 matches was a young Len Silver.

In spite of the pessimists fears that Foxhall Heath was too far outside Ipswich to attract the crowds, support was staggering. The ground record was smashed three times during the season and for the final league match against Rayleigh an astonishing gate of 19,000 was recorded. *Stenner's Annual* was able to report at the end of the 1953 season that 'Ipswich has become the No. 1 speedway stronghold'.

Bert Edwards, Harry Edwards' brother, appeared for Ipswich between 1953 and 1957.

Unlike Rayleigh, Ipswich revelled in the new Second Division when it began in 1954 and, with new signings Johnnie Chamberlain, Junior Bainbridge from Glasgow White City, Edinburgh's Dick Campbell and the Australian Bob Sharp, they set about the new opposition with relish, finishing the league in fifth place. At the end of the season, Ipswich took on Belle Vue in a special Second Division versus First Division challenge match in what was generally reckoned to be one of the most exciting meetings ever to take place at Foxhall. There was never more than four points separating the sides and with just one heat to go and the scores standing at 40-38 in Ipswich's favour, either side could have won the match. Ipswich were represented in the last race by Bob Sharp and Junior Bainbridge, while Ken Sharples and Don Cuppleditch lined up for Belle Vue. The race turned into a fierce duel between Sharp and Sharples for first place, with Sharples on the inside and Sharp riding round the boards. On the third lap it looked as though Sharp had lost control as he came dangerously near to the fence but he just managed to hang on. In the end Sharp seemed to find an extra turn of speed on the last bend and just held off Sharples by about a yard. With Bainbridge taking the third point, Ipswich held on to record a famous victory over First Division opposition by 44 points to 40. The biggest cheer of the night was reserved for Bert Edwards when he beat Peter Craven in the penultimate heat. The final night of the season saw an 18,500 strong crowd turn out to see Ipswich defeat Second Division champions Bristol by 52 points to 32.

Ipswich dropped one place in the table to sixth in 1955 after being undefeated at home and losing every match away. Bert Edwards and Junior Bainbridge again took the honours as top Witches: Edwards with an average of 12 points exactly and Bainbridge with an average of

10.6. Strangely enough, both men also finished the season as joint track record holders, with first of all Bainbridge on 14 July and then Edwards on 18 August setting a time of 71 seconds. Once again Ipswich proved to be the best supported team in Division Two with more than 16,000 spectators turning out to see the final match of the season.

Ipswich managed to improve their league position in 1956, finishing one place behind Rayleigh in fourth position. Ipswich fared even better in the Inter-Division League, managing to beat First Division opponents Norwich, Bradford and Belle Vue. Top scorers were once again captain Bert Edwards, Junior Bainbridge and Bob Sharp, all finishing the season with averages of over 10 points per match. In fact they finished sixth, eighth and ninth in the Second Division averages for 1956, the only team, apart from league champions Swindon to have three riders in the top ten. Bert Edwards was chosen to represent his country four times – three times against Australasia and once against Sweden – while Bob Sharp rode once for Australasia. Edwards also won the Sunday Pictorial South of England Challenge Cup at Southampton.

With the ending of the Second Division and their enforced promotion into speedway's top flight, Ipswich knew they needed to strengthen their team. As the 1957 season started they managed to do just that, signing two top-class heat leaders in Peter Moore and Cyril Roger, but unfortunately this was offset by injuries to Bert Edwards and Junior Bainbridge as well as to Cyril Roger himself, which kept them all out for a good part of the season. Norwegian star, Aage Hansen, was drafted in during September and was most impressive but only rode in a

Two of Ipswich's leading riders in the 1950s, Junior Bainbridge (left) and Bob Sharp (right) discuss tactics in the pits in 1957.

very few matches. Peter Moore was outstanding and recorded an average of 13.6, but this was not enough to save Ipswich and they finished just one place above Rayleigh at the foot of the league.

In complete contrast to Norwich, 1958 was to be Ipswich's most disastrous season in their history, as they finished bottom of the league with just three points – just one win and one draw in the entire season. Peter Moore was joined by two newcomers to the squad, Australian Ray Cresp and a young Nigel Boocock who had been left without a track following the demise of Birmingham. The only bright spot in the season was Peter Moore's qualification for the World Final.

Ipswich's appalling 1958 season left them with no alternative but to drop into the Southern Area League in 1959, this time under Aub Lawson's management. Although strong on paper, using riders such as Johnnie Chamberlain and Colin Gooddy, who proved to be outstanding in the league by averaging 10.8 for the season and winning the Silver Sash, Ipswich once again occupied the cellar position, winning just two matches at home and one away.

Ipswich's successful return to the top flight in 1960, after taking over Poole's licence, meant that for the first time in the history of speedway, Norwich did not finish the season as the top East Anglian team. Peter Moore and Ray Cresp came back to Foxhall Heath while the rest of the team consisted of Birger Forsberg, Jimmy Squibb, old Rayleigh favourites Jack Unstead and Les McGillivray, Colin Gooddy, Len Silver, and the veteran Jack Biggs. Ipswich came fourth in the league, while Norwich could only manage fifth.

The 1960 Ipswich team. From left to right, back row: Vic Gooden (promoter), Birger Forsberg, Peter Moore, Jack Unstead, Jimmy Squibb, Colin Gooddy, Maurice Littlechild (manager). Front row: Ray Cresp, Les McGillivray (captain, on bike), Len Silver.

Billy Bales of Norwich leads Jack Biggs, then riding for Poole before his move to Ipswich. Biggs will always be remembered as the man who snatched defeat from the jaws of victory in the 1951 World Championship final when, needing just one point from his last race to clinch the title, came last and then in the resulting run-off came last again.

Peter Moore's best ever season was probably 1960 as he finished with an average of 13.17 and came fourth in the World Championship. One race in particular that year which will always be remembered by those that saw it occurred on 25 August when Ipswich took on Southampton. Going into the final heat, Ipswich were just one point up. Moore was up against two of the top riders in the country – Bjorn Knutsson, who finished top of the averages that year, and Olle Nygren. Both were unbeaten and both had easily beaten Moore earlier in the meeting. But Moore knew the whole outcome of the match depended on him and he was ready. As the tapes flew up, Moore rocketed away and hit the first bend just in front. For four laps Knutsson and Nygren were on his exhaust pipe; at every bend one went inside and one went outside, but Moore just hung on. The crowd were going mad as for four electrifying, unbelievable laps, he hung on by the skin of his teeth. As they crossed the finishing line you could have covered all three with the proverbial handkerchief, but Moore was given the verdict and Ipswich won the match by one point.

Birger Forsberg flitted across the Ipswich scene leaving controversy in his wake. He had first ridden for Rayleigh in 1957, moved to Poole in 1958 and was called up by the Swedish Army in 1959, though he reappeared late in the season for Poole. Along with the rest of the team, he moved to Ipswich in 1960. Following a bad accident at New Cross he was laid up for several weeks and was never the same rider again; brilliant in patches, bumbling in others. Just in one night at New Cross, for example, he came from behind to beat Split Waterman, Jack Young and Peter Craven to win three separate heats, but he then fell off in his last two races. Another pile-up against Belle Vue saw him crack his backbone. He was then ordered by the

Swedish Control Board to ride in a league match in Sweden, but he refused as Ipswich also had a meeting that night. The Swedish Board took his licence away and he never rode again.

For the first time in many years, all ten of the National League clubs returned to race in 1961 and, although the Provincial League lost Yarmouth, Bradford and Liverpool, new teams in the shape of Plymouth, Exeter, Wolverhampton, Middlesbrough and Newcastle more than made up for their loss. Once again, Ipswich finished as top team in East Anglia, just one place above Norwich. Peter Moore had another good season, coming sixth in the league averages and beating Barry Briggs in an eliminator for the Match Race Championship, though, in the event, he was unable to take the Golden Helmet away from Ove Fundin. Moore received solid backing from Ray Cresp, Jack Unstead and Jimmy Squibb as well as South African newcomer, Trevor Blokdyk.

For 1962, new management took over at Foxhall Heath under Maurice Littlechild and Eric Bason. Peter Moore was back as were Colin Gooddy and Les McGillivray. The Swede, Leif Larsson, was brought in and turned out to be a real crowd-pleaser with his tearaway style and Split Waterman was signed from New Cross. Ray Cresp reluctantly returned from South Africa where he had been motor racing during the close season and told Eric Bason that he would only ride for Ipswich if he had no car racing bookings. He rode three times but then left for South Africa with his friend Trevor Blokdyk to continue his career in motor racing. Cresp was twenty-six before he took up speedway in Australia. Jack Biggs persuaded him to come to England at the end of the 1954/55 season. He rode in some second halves at Southampton before moving on to Eastbourne. He then signed up for Wembley and in 1957 he went to Oxford. Transferred to Ipswich for the 1958 season, he moved with the rest of the team to Poole in 1959 and back to Ipswich in 1960 when Vic Gooden took over. He qualified for the World Championship final in 1961 and later made a comeback, but for the time being he was lost to speedway.

The Witches started the season well, but were very soon losing heavily at home as well as away. They were routed by Southampton 60-18 and soundly beaten at home by Norwich. Another Swede, Bengt Brannefors, was brought in, but proved to be a complete flop and then broke his kneecap. On 16 July, Ipswich lost to Wimbledon by six points and the management decided to call it a day. Ipswich closed and speedway at Foxhall Heath temporarily finished. There was a suggestion that the National League promoters should help out by lending the club £100 each, with the cash being paid back out of Ipswich's share of the World Championship final profits. Vic Gooden offered to take over the licence from Eric Bason, but neither of these suggestions were acceptable to the Control Board.

The 1962 season was when handicapping was tried out. The big five – Fundin, Briggs, Craven, Moore and Knutsson – had to start 20 yards back, other full team members started 10 yards back, while reserves went off scratch. Moore and Cresp were both very slick gaters who liked to win their races from the front, so this presented them with some difficulties. Moore adapted, but Cresp never did. Waterman decided it was time to call it a day and, although Colin Gooddy showed a big improvement, the fact was that Ipswich were really down to just one recognised heat leader. Having won their first two home matches, they then proceeded to lose the next five. By July the writing was on the wall.

The death of former Rayleigh and Ipswich favourite, Jack Unstead, was a tragic event that occurred in 1962. Jack had left Ipswich to take his chance in the Provincial League with

Left: *Birger Forsberg only appeared for Ipswich in one season (1960), but it was steeped in controversy.* Right: *The slick gating Aussie, Ray Cresp, seen here wearing Poole colours, rode for Ipswich in 1960, 1961 and very briefly in 1962, before deciding that he would rather race cars. He returned for another season in 1965.*

Exeter, but had turned out for Ipswich during 1962 as a replacement for Cresp. On 13 April, almost thirteen years to the day after he started his racing career, Jack met with his fatal accident while racing for Exeter against Southampton.

It was reported at the end of 1962 that former rider 'Skid' Parish had acquired the stadium and intended to organise a training school during the winter.

Foxhall stadium opened its doors again in 1964 to run a series of open meetings and later ran a team in the Metropolitan League. The Ipswich team consisted of Ron Bagley as captain, Brian Davies, David Crane, Derek Battle and Ray Cousins. Many of the Ipswich and Rayleigh riders also held down team places in full Provincial League teams. Bagley, for example, was riding for Sheffield, Crane for Exeter, Edwards for Wolverhampton, Hitch for Middlesbrough and Ridgeon for Glasgow. During the 1964/65 winter, John Pilblad and Ken Vale ran a training school at Ipswich while efforts were made to bring top level speedway back to Foxhall.

Like Rayleigh, Ipswich applied for an open licence in 1965 with a view to operating in the new British League in 1966, but they fared little better than Rayleigh, managing just four meetings, including one that was rained off. Lack of competitive speedway was blamed as the reason for their abortive season.

In 1969 there was a continued expansion in speedway as the British League First Division continued with nineteen teams, but the Second Division increased from ten to sixteen, which included the return of Ipswich and an entry from King's Lynn's second team, the Starlets.

It was two newcomers to the promoting game, Joe Thurley and John Berry, who had decided to try their hand at reviving Ipswich. They brought in John Harrhy, Pete Bailey, Ted Spittles, former Ipswich and Yarmouth rider Ron Bagley, Ernie Baker and Neville Slee and entered the Second Division full of optimism and hope. Twice in the last decade, Ipswich had had to close through lack of support, so it was with an element of fingers crossed that the new co-promoters waited to see the size of the crowd on their opening night. The new promoters were said to be disappointed when 3,000 turned up. When Ipswich lost that opening match they thought they had made a big mistake, when they lost their second home match they wondered whether it was worth continuing. In all, Ipswich lost every one of their first five matches, but things gradually began to improve and, although the Witches did not set the League alight in that first season when they finished eleventh, they did enough to show that Ipswich were back and here to stay.

It was also in 1969 that a young man by the name of John Louis was approached and asked if he would like to have a go at speedway. In spite of being a top local scrambler, Louis was very reluctant to have a go. In the end he agreed to a trial session on condition that it was held

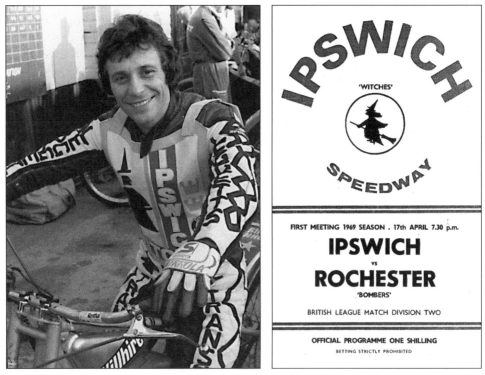

Left: *John Louis, the British speedway sensation of 1970, finished his first season in speedway as Ipswich's top scorer.* Right: *Programme cover for the first meeting of Ipswich's return to league speedway in 1969 after a lay-off of four years.*

after a meeting; that all the stadium lights had to be turned off for ten minutes so that all the spectators would leave and then, and only then, would he try his hand. All the conditions were met, but Louis got scared and joined the crowd by going home instead! Eventually, he was persuaded to ride in a second-half event and the rest, as they say, is history.

East Anglia had to look to Ipswich for success in 1970 as the Witches came on by leaps and bounds thanks, in the main, to John Harrhy and sensational new discovery John Louis, who, following his reluctant second-half debut the year before, had spent the winter practising at Olle Nygren's training school at King's Lynn. His debut in British League racing was nothing short of sensational and he rocketed onto the scene like a thunderbolt, scoring seven points in each of his first two matches. He finished the season as top points scorer, with 7 full and 1 paid maximums under his belt, which was some going for a rider who had never ridden in a single league match in his life before. He also took the Silver Helmet in August and successfully defended it seven times to end the season as holder. With solid support from Pete Bailey and Ron Bagley, the team finished sixth in the league, but their greatest triumph was in winning the Knock-Out Cup, beating Berwick in the final by 82 points to 74.

With John Louis now firmly established in the team, Ipswich were looking for great things in 1971 and sure enough Ipswich's rise to the top continued, but not half as much as John Louis'. It was a phenomenal year for the youngster, who it has to be remembered was still only in his second year of competitive racing. In 38 matches for the Witches he recorded an unbelievable 21 full and 4 paid maximums to finish the season with an incredible average of 11.31, easily topping the averages for the division. He commenced the season as holder of the Silver Helmet and successfully defended it 25 times, losing it once mid-season and regaining it before losing it at the end of the season to Phil Crump. To cap it all he won the Division Two Riders' Championship.

As if one exceptional youngster wasn't enough, Ipswich unearthed another in Tony Davey. He had ridden in just four matches in 1970, making 1971 his first full season. He too topped 400 points with 9 full and 4 paid maximums, finishing with an average of 9.93. If Ipswich went on finding talent like this, what chance was there for the rest of the league? Fortunately for them, at least in 1971, the only real backing for these two outstanding youngsters came from Pete Bailey and so Ipswich, in the end, could only manage third place.

The 1972 season started off with the big news that Ipswich had decided to seek, and had been granted, Division One status by obtaining West Ham's licence when they pulled out of the league. Ipswich, under their new manager and former rider Ron Bagley, knew that if they continued in Division Two they would lose John Louis, who was so obviously ready for the big time. In his first year in the top flight, Louis finished with an average of 9.39. As a Division One rider he also now entered the World Championship for the first time. Incredibly, not only did he reach the final, but he scored 11 points and finished joint fourth ahead of such established world-class stars as Anders Michanek, Nigel Boocock and Barry Briggs.

Around Louis, Bagley built a first-class team, retaining Tony Davey and bringing in Olle Nygren and Alan Sage from the defunct West Ham as well as Tommy Johansson, Sandor Levai and the sixteen-year-old Australian youngster, Billy Sanders. Surely Ipswich's latest youngster could not follow in the same mould as their other discoveries…

The team finished a creditable sixth in the league with the two Swedes, Nygren and Johansson, providing solid support to Louis. But, for the third year running, the real story of Ipswich lay in the continued rise and rise of Mr Ipswich himself, John 'Tiger' Louis.

The news at Ipswich in 1973 was once again made by their youngsters. Louis, almost unbelievably, managed to improve his average, as did Tony Davey, and the seventeen-year-old Billy Sanders moved up to become the third heat leader with an average of 7.43. They completely dominated the team and left question marks hanging over the older members such as Olle Nygren and Sandor Levai. If they had been able to provide the necessary support then Ipswich would have been in with a chance of league honours. As it was the Witches finished fifth and once again looked to the future. Tony Davey managed to win the Golden Helmet but lost it at his first defence. Louis won it from Reidar Eide on 17 May, lost it to him the following night, regained it on 13 September from Arnold Haley and retained it through five challenges to end the season as holder.

Following his fourth place in the 1972 World Championship, there were great hopes at Foxhall that Louis might go at least one better and get a tractor ride this year. However, his challenge ended in controversy when he was banned from taking part in the European Final following a random fuel check at the British Nordic Final in which it was found that the fuel he had used contained a prohibited additive. He was cleared by the Speedway Control Board when it was discovered that it was an accident by the fuel suppliers and did not assist his performance in any way. He was given the go-ahead to appear in the European Final but with only hours to go before the opening ceremony, the FIM banned him again and he was forced

A third teenage sensation came along in the form of sixteen-year-old Billy Sanders, seen here in action in Sydney.

Left: *Following in John Louis' footsteps, Ipswich unearthed another teenage sensation in Tony Davey.* Right: *Billy Sanders was the only Ipswich rider to feature in all three league winning teams of 1975, 1976 and 1984.*

to withdraw. It was a sad end to his World Championship bid and when you remember that the winner that year was Jerzy Szczakiel, the little known Polish rider, who knows what might have happened if Louis had been allowed to compete.

Ipswich moved up from fifth place to third in 1974, thanks yet again to the Louis, Davey, Sanders triumvirate. They received excellent support from the rest of the team, who, after Nygren left in mid-season following a disagreement over the state of the track for the Witches home match with Wimbledon, which he felt was too dangerous to ride, were all products of a policy of bringing on home-grown talent. Individually, John Louis continued on his majestic way, reaching his second World Championship final where, once again, he came fourth. He started the season as holder of the Golden Helmet, which had reverted to its old format for 1974, and finished the season unbeaten, having seen off challenges from Ray Wilson, Peter Collins, Malcolm Simmons, Dag Lovaas, Ole Olsen and Phil Crump. Billy Sanders continued his improvement, becoming one of the few riders that season to score over 400 points. The scene was set for Ipswich's glory years…

Ipswich started the 1975 season concerned about the mammoth increases in the price of petrol. Foxhall Heath was some way outside Ipswich and also drew a large following from rural areas around Suffolk and North Essex. John Berry and Ron Bagley were worried that petrol prices would put supporters off and so their solution was to get Eastern Counties

Kevin Jolly and Billy Sanders take the inside line against Bernie Leigh and Dave Jessup of Reading.

Omnibus Company to run special buses from places like Halesworth, Felixstowe, Stowmarket and Hadleigh. If getting supporters to the track was of some concern, what they saw when they got there was of no concern at all. The team, which was full of home-grown talent, carried all before them. Ipswich used just eight riders during the whole season, all products of their own training: John Louis, Billy Sanders, Tony Davey, Mike Lanham, Mick Hines, Trevor Jones, Ted Howgego and Dave Gooderham. They swept to victory in the league for the first time in Ipswich's history.

The season started fairly quietly with wins at home and losses away. In June they put together a run of five away wins, lost at Belle Vue and Sheffield and then, from August 23 until the end of the season, they never lost another match either home or away. The end of the season was nail-biting stuff for the team and their supporters. Needing to win away at Halifax in their last match of the season to stand any chance of the title, they did just that. However, they then had to wait two days as the only team that could overtake them, Belle Vue, were due to race at Exeter. A win there and the title would belong to the Aces, but it was not to be and Ipswich were the champions. Not only was this done with all home-grown riders but Ipswich absolutely refused to use guest riders on the few occasions when they could have, though this was not very often as Louis, Sanders, Lanham, Hines and Jones appeared in every single league and cup match. Louis again scored at over 10 points a match, while Sanders backed him up with 352 points from 36 matches. The season finished on an even higher note for Louis as he went one better than his fourth place in the World Championship, claiming a place on the rostrum. The first English rider to do so since Peter Craven's victory in 1962, he had had to beat four times World Champion Ivan Mauger in a run-off to do it.

How could 1976 be any better for Ipswich? Well, they could win the Knock-Out Cup which had eluded them even in their all-conquering 1975 campaign. The only problem was that John Louis missed eight league matches due to a dislocated shoulder and, as was well known, John Berry refused to use guest riders. To help him over the crisis, the Ipswich promoter drafted in some new blood – Kevin Jolly, Andy Hines and Colin Cook – who were again all local products. Of the eight matches Ipswich rode without John Louis, they won five and lost three. When Louis returned for the last fifteen matches of the season, they won fourteen and lost just one. Ipswich did go one better, winning the league by seven clear points and taking the Knock-Out Cup by 91 points to 63 over local rivals, King's Lynn. Strangely enough, the one major trophy Ipswich did not win was the Inter-Divisional Knock-Out Cup. In what was the most sensational result of the 1976 season, Ipswich travelled to National League team Workington with a full side and lost 40-38. Workington proved it was no fluke by going on to beat King's Lynn by the same score in the quarter-finals.

Once again Louis qualified for the World Championship final and, although an Englishman won the title for the first time since 1962, it was Peter Collins of Belle Vue and not Louis. Louis finished sixth on 9 points. Louis' consolation was to partner Malcolm Simmons to victory in Eskilstuna in the World Pairs, scoring 17 out of a possible 18 points. Billy Sanders also tasted his share of world honours that year, when he rode in Australia's victorious World Team Championship team at White City, scoring seven points. Sanders had

Mike Lanham, another local discovery, rode for Ipswich from 1972 to 1982.

been a major influence in getting Australia through to their first ever final, scoring a 12 point maximum in the British qualifying round at Ipswich.

Could Ipswich do it again in 1977? They kept the same team of home-grown products together and added another in Nigel Flatman. The customary team was the same as the year before: John Louis, Billy Sanders, Tony Davey, Mike Lanham, Ted Howgego, Kevin Jolly and Dave Gooderham. All of them held their form and yet it was not to be as Ipswich finally finished the season in fourth place with a total of 25 wins out of 36 matches. This number of wins would have been enough to win the British League in 1965, 1967, 1968, 1971, 1973 and 1974. The fact was that it was not that Ipswich had deteriorated but that other teams had strengthened their squads.

In spite of dropping three positions in the league, Ipswich were only four points behind the winners White City and John Berry knew he was still right to persevere with his policy of bringing on his own talent and refusing to use guest riders.

For the first time since he arrived like an express train on the Foxhall Heath scene, John Louis was not the top scorer. This was Billy Sanders' year. Both averaged just under 11 points at home, but it was Sanders' away form that made the difference: he averaged 9.89, whereas Louis could only manage 8.5. It was also Sanders' turn to reach the World Final – his first – where he scored 6 points and came ninth. Louis failed to get past the British Final.

Ipswich made just one adjustment for their 1978 line-up, bringing in Colin Cook to replace Dave Gooderham. There were other important changes as, firstly, Olle Nygren was appointed team manager and, secondly, John Louis volunteered to give up the number one race jacket in favour of Billy Sanders. With Sanders topping the averages in 1977 it was felt that he was now the right man to take on the top opposition in heat one while Louis, riding at number five, would be able to use his experience to keep an eye on the lower order riders. The top three were yet again firing on all cylinders, with Sanders recording an average of 10.23 and Tony Davey overtaking Louis for second place with 9.44. With the exception of Kevin Jolly though, the rest of the team did not quite enjoy as much success as they had the previous year with the result that Ipswich slipped down the table to sixth place. John Berry, forsaking his local grown talent only policy, slipped into the transfer market late in the season and signed up West German George Hack, whose inclusion brought about such a revival that Ipswich went on to win the Knock-Out Cup final for the second time in three years.

In 1979, Ipswich sunk to the depths of fifteenth place, just three years after the heights of being champions. The Ipswich junior talent conveyor belt was drying up, with the banning of Ipswich riders from using the training facilities at Mildenhall not helping matters. Billy Sanders decided to seek pastures new and Tony Davey's form was well down on the previous three years. Ipswich tried to make up for these deficiencies by signing Scandinavians Preben Eriksen and former World Champion, Anders Michanek, but neither of them proved to be the answer. The return of Billy Sanders from Birmingham late in the season boosted their hopes for 1980.

There were two bright spots in an otherwise forgettable season. The first was the return to top-class form of John Louis – not that he had ever really been anything else, but 1978 had not been quite so prolific for him. The second was the decision by Ipswich Council to once more allow two hours of practice per fortnight. It was following the cancellation of this practice session that Ipswich's fall from the top of the league had begun. John Louis' return

The 1983 Ipswich team. From left to right: Billy Sanders, Nigel Flatman, Andy Hibbs, Dennis Sigalos, Andy Hines, Jeremy Doncaster, Preben Eriksen.

to form saw him win the British League Riders' Championship and be appointed England captain for 1980. It was enough to gain him recognition outside the sport as well as he was named Ipswich Professional Sports Personality of the Year ahead of Ipswich Town Football Club's Dutch star, Arnold Muhren. This was some achievement when the speedway team were pulling in crowds of 6,000-8,000 compared to football's 20,000.

Ipswich had a better year in 1980 than their poor 1979, but it was becoming evident that the old triumvirate of Louis, Sanders and Davey were beginning to score less freely. Louis and Sanders, although continuing to do well individually (as their results in the World Championship showed), nevertheless could only manage 8.67 and 8.65 respectively in the league, while Tony Davey dropped right down to 6.0 and actually occupied sixth place in the team's overall averages. Kevin Jolly, in nine matches, managed 9.18 to top the averages, while Mike Lanham and Preben Eriksen both outscored Davey. The fact that Louis, Sanders and Davey were all dropping points led John Berry to a radical rethink of his home-grown policy. As the season ended he sold Louis to Halifax, Sanders went to Hull and, in exchange, Ipswich brought in two Americans, Dennis Sigalos and John Cook. It was the end of an era at Foxhall Heath. Yet, in spite of this rethink, Ipswich had just won the Anglia Junior League for the second time in three years, this time losing only 2 out of 16 matches and pushing Mildenhall into second place.

The big question for 1981 was, would the new look Ipswich bring back the glory days of the mid-70s to Foxhall? The answer was so very nearly yes, as the two new American signings led the Witches into second place in the league behind an all-conquering Cradley Heath team and to first place in the reconstituted Speedway Star Knock-Out Cup, having defeated

Cradley Heath in the quarter-final. It seemed after all that John Berry's bold move in letting Louis and Sanders go had been a masterstroke and yet at the beginning of the season it appeared to many observers that he had been very foolish. There was no argument about the arrival of Dennis Sigalos as he was a recognised top-notch rider, but John Cook? He arrived from Hull with an average of 4.04 and took the reserve spot. His first match in Witches colours saw him score 4 points from 4 starts, in his second match he got 5 from 4 but, though the points were not flowing freely, everyone was very impressed by his never-give-up attitude and his whole-hearted commitment. His breakthrough finally came in a League Cup match at Hackney on 17 April where he scored 14 points from 6 starts and from then on he was always challenging Sigalos for top spot.

While the two Americans were having their own private battle, the rest of the team were giving solid backing and at one point in the season they went through fourteen matches unbeaten and then finished the season with a further run of six unbeaten matches. As was usual when Ipswich did well, it was partly because they had a settled team. Only eight riders were used throughout the league campaign and even then Andy Hines only rode in one match, leaving Sigalos, Cook, Kevin Jolly, Mike Lanham, Preben Eriksen and Nigel Flatman as ever-presents, with Tim Hunt missing just one match. Kevin Jolly fulfilled the promise of the previous season by confirming his place as third heat leader, just ahead of Eriksen on 7.32. Nigel Flatman justified Ipswich's faith in recalling him from Mildenhall by finishing the season with a 6.02 average. Sigalos and Cook also represented USA in Test matches during 1981, Cook averaging 7.8 from 3 matches, Sigalos 6.00 from 5.

If the mid-1970s were a golden age for the Witches then the early '80s, under the inspired leadership of the two Americans, were to prove most definitely a silver age. Following their

Dennis Sigalos was Ipswich's leading rider from 1981 to 1983. He returned for a short spell in 1985.

John Cook tries to go round Kevin Smith of Poole.

success in 1981, Ipswich maintained their assault on the league championship in 1982, eventually finishing third behind Belle Vue and Cradley Heath. Sigalos improved on his previous year's performance, finishing with an average of 10.10, while Preben Eriksen leapfrogged John Cook to become Ipswich's second heat leader and ever-presents Kevin Jolly and Nigel Flatman provided strong support with 6.99 and 5.79 respectively.

The signing of twenty-two-year-old European 250cc grass track champion Jeremy Doncaster in the early months of 1982 was an event that was to have far-reaching and long-standing effects on the club. With no speedway experience whatsoever, Doncaster was slotted straight into the team. John Berry saw nothing wrong in this: 'Putting Jeremy straight into the team is not a gamble,' he said. Berry was right as Doncaster showed great promise in his first ever season, finishing with an average of 6.07.

The year ended on a high note for Sigalos as, for the first time ever, the World Championship final was held in America and he finished third behind fellow American Bruce Penhall and England's Les Collins.

Ipswich's silver age continued in 1983 as they welcomed back one of their mid-1970s stars, Billy Sanders. Sanders replaced Cook and improved on the latter's 1982 average by two points per match. This, and Jeremy Doncaster's rise to heat leader status, pushed Ipswich one place up the table to finish runners-up to top-of-the-table Cradley. Cradley had a tremendous season, setting a new British League record by losing just two matches, one of those to Ipswich.

Dennis Sigalos had another brilliant season, averaging 10.75 per match, but it was Billy Sanders who stole the individual honours, finishing runner-up in the World Championship

Preben Eriksen gave solid support to Ipswich's top stars from 1979 until 1983.

final. Sanders also represented the Witches in the British League Riders' Championship, finishing sixth, one place behind his former captain and team-mate, John Louis, now riding for neighbours King's Lynn.

The silver age at Ipswich at last turned to gold in 1984 as the Witches carried all before them to win the league championship for the first time since 1976. For good measure they also won the Knock-Out Cup. The inspiration for this success was once again provided by Billy Sanders, who was the only rider to have ridden in all three league championship winning teams of 1975, 1976 and 1984. Sigalos had left, to be replaced by fellow American and former Witch, John Cook, while Jeremy Doncaster made the third heat leader spot most definitely his. Two newcomers, Finland's Kai Niemi and Richard Knight, both gave solid support with averages of over seven points per match. Completing the double winning line-up were Nigel Flatman, now in his eighth season with the Witches and Carl Blackbird, newly arrived from National League Mildenhall. The strength of the team could be seen by the fact that six of the team scored maximums during the year, with only Blackbird missing out, while Sanders and Cook managed nine apiece.

The 1985 season started with great promise for Ipswich as John Louis had returned as manager. However, one of the greatest tragedies ever to befall speedway, let alone East Anglian speedway, occurred on 23 April 1985. It was, in John Berry's words, 'the blackest day in the history of Ipswich speedway'. It was on that day that the twenty-nine-year-old Billy Sanders, the inspiration behind Ipswich's league successes, was found dead in the front seat of a friend's car parked in the woods near Foxhall Heath stadium. A length of tubing running from the exhaust to the inside of the car showed it was no accident. Billy Sanders had committed suicide. It was later learned that his nine-year marriage had just ended. At the time of his death, Sanders was averaging 11.53 per match for the Witches.

Nothing else mattered for Ipswich that season, but they put on a brave display and managed to finish in fifth place. They even reached the final of the Knock-Out Cup, losing by just three points to league champions Oxford. Ipswich met Oxford a total of eight times that season – in the British League, the Knock-Out Cup and the League Cup – and although Oxford did the League and Cup double, Ipswich were beaten only three times in the eight meetings. Without Sanders, it was left to new captain John Cook and Jeremy Doncaster to inspire the team and they had strong support from the ever-improving Richard Knight, who forced his way into the third heat leader position with an average of 8.56. Kai Niemi was brought back to replace Sanders. John Cook had to return to America for the American Championship in June. It was just as well for him that he did because he won with a faultless maximum, beating Sam Ermolenko into second place. On his return to Foxhall he complained about the condition of the track, a disagreement with John Berry that was to fester for the rest of the season.

Co-promoter Chris Shears pulled off a major coup late in the season when he re-signed former Ipswich favourite, Dennis Sigalos, from Wolverhampton. However, his first match back in Witches colours saw him involved in a horrendous accident against Reading, which fortunately looked much worse than it was and he carried on with just a few cuts and bruises.

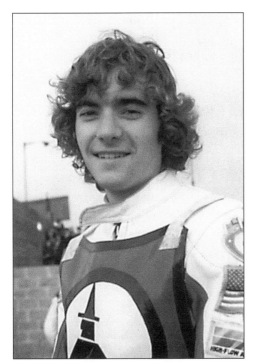 

Left: *Dennis Sigalos came third in the 1982 World Championship.* Right: *John Cook was an outstanding rider for Ipswich between 1981 and 1985, but he had his ups and downs with the management!*

The season ended on a somewhat sour note as, with one heat to go in the Knock-Out Cup final, Ipswich needed a 5-1 to lift the cup, but Cook and Doncaster managed to get in each other's way and the trophy headed Cowley's way. This incident provoked another argument between Cook and Berry, with Cook claiming that Berry was putting undue pressure on the riders, while Berry accused Cook of letting the side down. In his end of season comments in the programme for Ipswich's last home match of the season, Berry wrote: 'John [Cook] is an exceptionally naturally talented speedway rider, which, encourages the theory that everyone has at least one saving grace. Other than that, as my old headmaster wrote in my last school report, I prefer not to comment.' This was, however, to be John Berry's last season in charge of Ipswich as he stepped down and handed the reins over to Chris Shears at the end of the season.

Since promotion to Division One in 1972, Ipswich had won the league three times, been runners-up twice and third twice. They had also won the Knock-Out Cup on four occasions and been runners-up twice, all under the expert guidance of John Berry. When John Berry had first applied for a licence to run Ipswich in the Second Division along with Joe Thurley, he was turned down because it was felt he did not have enough experience!

Both John Cook and Kai Niemi reached the final of the World Championship, Cook coming seventh with 9 points, while the unfancied Niemi did even better, finishing fourth with 10. Perhaps he would have done even better had it not been for his injuries. He had crashed heavily in the British League match against Swindon, badly damaging his ankle, and had to limp his way through the Inter-Continental final with the aid of crutches. In great distress, he rode again in the World Final, where his 10 points came from his first four rides. Erik Gundersen won the title with 13 points. Who knows what a fully fit Niemi might have done? The 1985 season had certainly been an eventful one for Ipswich.

In sole charge for the first time, Chris Shears looked forward to the 1986 season with a great deal of optimism. True, Kai Niemi had left, but in his place Ipswich had signed up Jens Rasmussen on loan from Oxford and Louis Carr for £10,000 from Ellesmere Port. With Jeremy Doncaster, John Cook and Richard Knight making up the rest of the team and with promising youngsters Alan Farmer and Robbie Fuller as reserves, there seemed to be every reason to believe that this could again be the Witches' season. A massive 52-25 victory over King's Lynn in an early season challenge match served only to confirm this optimism. The first sign of trouble occurred when John Cook failed to turn up at Odsal because of a dispute over terms. After much wrangling, and only four matches in Witches colours, Cook returned to America, taking no further part in Ipswich's campaign that year. Eventually, in August, Niemi returned to take Cook's place.

Further internal problems were to come when John Louis resigned as manager after the visit of Coventry. There had been disagreements between him and Shears over several aspects of management. John Berry briefly stepped into the breach to cover the manager's duties.

Only Jeremy Doncaster could really look back on the season with any satisfaction as his average went up to 10.38, firmly establishing him as Ipswich's number one. He also won the Golden Helmet from Kenny Carter and made three successful defences before losing it to Sam Ermolenko. He then regained it from reigning World Champion, Erik Gundersen, lost it and once more regained it from Gundersen before finally losing it on 25 September. The team finished the season ninth out of eleven teams and lost in the first round of the Knock-Out Cup.

King's Lynn's Dave Jessup tries to go inside Dennis Sigalos. This image comes from the 1981 clash between Ipswich and King's Lynn.

Chris Shears moved quickly to strengthen the Witches in time for the 1987 season. Jamie Luckhurst was signed from National League Wimbledon, where he had been top scorer with an average of 9.83 and considered one of the hottest properties in the League, ready and able enough for promotion to the British League. Inexplicably, he struggled in Ipswich colours and, after 12 matches, had an average of just 2.20 to show for his efforts. The team itself was also suffering, having finished bottom of the British League Cup table. Shears then signed up Martin Hagon from Sheffield to take Luckhurst's place, and Luckhurst moved back to the National League with Rye House. Shears also signed up two foreign riders in the shape of Italy's Armando Castagna and Gerd Riss from Germany, and with Jeremy Doncaster and Kai Niemi still scoring well, Ipswich got themselves into gear at last, finishing up sixth in the British League table. Not brilliant, but better than it looked at one time.

For the first time ever, the World Championship final was held over two days, with the scores of both meetings counting towards the final score. Both Jeremy Doncaster and Gerd Riss qualified for the final. Doncaster scored a total of 20 points to finish sixth, while Riss scored 12 and came tenth. Doncaster also regained the Golden Helmet in April and successfully defended it twice.

The final few weeks of the 1987 season had left Ipswich full of hope for 1988. They had lost just three of their final fixtures and in Jeremy Doncaster, Armando Castagna, Kai Niemi and Gerd Riss had a good basis for the year to come. Chris Shears knew he would need to juggle around the lower reaches of the team and make a few more signings to be in with a chance of the title and he set about doing just that. Then, as if a forerunner of the sort of luck that was to dog Ipswich all season, the Speedway Control Board stepped in and banned the Witches from making any transfers, alleging debts accrued in the previous year. Shears protested and in the end the BSPA resolved the issue. Shears moved quickly and signed up Carl Blackbird from Belle Vue and Steve Regeling from King's Lynn.

Two of Ipswich's top stars of the eighties, Kai Niemi (left) and Jeremy Doncaster.

With only two matches behind them Ipswich lost Regeling, who broke two fingers in a crash with Bo Petersen at King's Lynn. Armando Castagna then injured his back and tore a kidney after crashing heavily against Coventry. A week later it was Blackbird's turn. Regeling left Ipswich altogether to be replaced by another Italian, Paolo Salvatelli, who crashed in practice. Kai Niemi was carried unconscious from a World Team Cup round in Germany and Riss decided to quit after a disappointing Continental Final. The ill luck went on and on all season. With just one week to go before the end of the season, Jeremy Doncaster crashed. By the time the season had come to an end Ipswich had used the incredible number of thirty different riders including Chris Louis, son of John, on loan from Hackney, as well as ten guests. The season came to a fitting end when the last meeting, the GM/Trevor Hedge 16-Lapper, was called off due to a lack of riders. Amazingly, Ipswich managed to avoid finishing bottom of the League, coming one place above the wooden-spoonists, Bradford. Although skipper Jeremy Doncaster still managed to top the averages with 9.34, he made an early exit from the World Championship as did fellow former finalists Gerd Riss and Kai Niemi. Doncaster was Ipswich's representative at the British League Riders' Championship final, where he came last, failing to score any points at all.

As if all this wasn't bad enough, Spedeworth, the owners of Foxhall Heath Stadium, made it known that they no longer wanted Shears to promote speedway. Company spokesman John Earry said that Spedeworth were in negotiations with several other parties including Skid Parish. They cited two reasons for being unhappy with Shears. One was that the stadium was not being cleaned up after meetings, the second was that drainage work had not been carried out satisfactorily. At the end of the season, after Shears called off the 16-Lapper, Spedeworth added the complaint that Shears had contracted to run a minimum of thirty meetings and he hadn't run them. Could things get much worse?

After protracted negotiations, which involved Hackney, Mildenhall and Reading as well as Ipswich, it was Hackney promoter Dave Pavitt who took over the Witches for 1989, dropping down to the National League and installing John Louis and Mike Western as promoters, with Louis as team manager. Shears, having unsuccessfully bid for Mildenhall, left with Jeremy Doncaster, Carl Blackbird and Armando Castagna for Reading. The new promoters brought with them three of the successful double winning 1988 Hackney side in Mark Loram, Alan Mogridge and Chris Louis. Dean Standing was signed from Eastbourne, local rider Robbie Fuller stayed on and Ipswich already had the makings of a title winning team. In spite of the drop in league status, the supporters were looking froward to another successful season and sponsorship flooded in, with Hunting Hire becoming the main backers.

The dream team got off to a faltering start as, in their very first match at home, they went down by one point to Poole. To the home team it was like an away fixture as it was the first time most of them had ridden a competitive match at Foxhall, but it was to be their only home defeat of the season. In the end, Ipswich finished fourth and got knocked out of the cup in the second round, but there were compensations: Mark Loram won the National League Riders' Championship, John Louis and Western were named Promoters of the Year and they were also presented with the Best Prepared Track award. Both Loram and Chris Louis finished the season with nine plus averages, while Standing finished with 8.20. This was also the first time in twelve seasons that Nigel Flatman had not ridden for the Witches.

It was too much to hope that Mark Loram would stay in the National League for another season and so it proved as Ipswich transferred one of the brightest young British stars to

Left: *Ipswich's Finnish star, Kai Niemi, joined the club in 1984 and stayed until 1988.* Right: *Italy's top rider, Armando Castagna, joined Ipswich in 1987 for a couple of seasons.*

appear on the scene for some time to King's Lynn for £20,000. In his place though, the Ipswich management signed David Norris for £15,000 and brought over the hot Australian prospect, Shane Parker.

For a while it seemed as though 1990 would be Ipswich's year – until they visited Exeter! At the end of this encounter, David Norris and Dean Standing found themselves in the Royal Devon and Exeter Hospital and both missed the following night's encounter with Poole. Norris also missed a lot more besides. Although Standing returned quicker than Norris, he never seemed to recover his form. Ever-presents Chris Louis and skipper Alan Mogridge tried their best, but the support proved not to be there in the end and, although the Witches finished in a respectable third place in the league, it was still something of a disappointment after their flying start. Chris Louis topped the averages with 10.18 and looked to be every bit as good a prospect as Mark Loram. He also finished runner-up in the National League Riders' Championship to Andy Grahame.

With the British League now down to nine teams and the National League up to 17 it was felt that the time was right to amalgamate them into the British League Divisions One and Two to even up the sizes. Automatic promotion and relegation were also introduced (something Norwich had campaigned for back in the forties) so, as 1991 started, the top teams from the old National League found themselves promoted into the British League Division One. Amongst those teams was Ipswich, who realised that they would have to do some strengthening if they were to live with the big boys. Certainly Chris Louis, David Norris and Shane Parker had done enough to show that they were worthy of a team place, but other changes were needed. Eventually, John Louis looked abroad and signed up a promising young Swede by the name of Tony Rickardsson and the Czechoslovakian Zdenek (Sam to his friends) Tesar, who had managed to reach the 1990 World Final, where he had scored 2 points and finished equal thirteenth. Promising local junior, Ben Howe, who led the Ipswich Juniors in the Reserves' League, also came into the team. Midway through the season Neville Tatum joined them, on loan from Eastbourne.

The Witches thrived back in the top division under the captaincy of Chris Louis and finished the season in seventh place, as well as winning the HEAT Team Division One Championship. At an individual level, the Ipswich riders showed what they were capable of on the wider stage. Ben Howe won the Reserves' League Championship, Shane Parker came fourth in the World Under-21 Final, Chris Louis represented England in four Test matches during the year as well as representing England in the World Team Cup final and Tony Rickardsson finished runner-up in the World Championship. Ipswich were once again producing a team of top names and looked set for big things in 1992.

With the exception of Neville Tatum, recalled by Eastbourne, Ipswich managed to keep their team together. In Tatum's place, Louis signed up one of Poland's hottest young discoveries, Jacek Rempala. With Chris Louis and Tony Rickardsson leading from the front, Sam Tesar as third heat leader and the ever improving Shane Parker, David Norris and Ben Howe behind them, Ipswich were hoping for real improvements from their seventh position in the League. However, 1992 turned out to be more a year of consolidation than improvement as the Witches rose just one place in the table to sixth spot. Rempala was a big disappointment and was let go after just four matches, his place being taken by Tony Olsson, who was signed up from Exeter. Ipswich were given a lot of hope for the future by

Witch Reminds Me ...

Issue Nº 5 - Original Date 5/2/91

Amalgamation Or Bust?

ONLY
20p

Welcome to Issue 5 of Witch Reminds Me ..., the only environmentally friendly speedway fanzine - printed in full colour on 100% recycled paper - bringing you:

- **a look at the amalgamation and related issues**
- **gossip, rumours, hearsay, scandal and tittle-tattle**
- **what to do to get your garden ready for the summer**
- **honest views from the people that count - THE FANS**

Slightly earlier than planned, but that's because there's so much going on.

Witch Reminds Me ... is totally independent from Ipswich Speedway Promotions and the Ipswich Speedway Supporters Club, and is indebted to everyone in Speedway for their collective but varied inspiration.

Thanks must go to all who have helped to keep Witch Reminds Me ... going through the winter months, especially those of you who subscribed. Further details of how to continue receiving WRM ... can be found inside.

Editor: Roger Jacobs
Contributors: Ryan Nodung, Dr B D Marten, Sid Winters

All proceeds from the sale of this fanzine go to help the Ipswich Witches Junior Team

Oo-er, there does seem to be a lot of serious content in this issue, but that's the way the cookie crumbles. Although much of the speedway press and many of the promoters seem to think that the Stewksbury amalgamation is the best thing since sliced bread, there are still lots of unanswered questions. Also, there are plenty of fans who are very suspicious of what has happened and *might* happen. The supporters voices must be heard - they are the people who pay the money, to be entertained. The sincere hope, of course, is that WRM ... won't have to turn round at the end of the 1991 season and say "We told you so".

Left: *Loyal team man, Nigel Flatman, rode for Ipswich for twelve seasons, from 1977 to 1988.* Right: Witch Reminds Me, *one of Ipswich's unofficial fanzines. This one reported the fact that Ipswich had met King's Lynn fifteen times during the 1988 season!*

the performance of their reserve team who swept all before them in the Reserves' League, losing just 1 match out of 23, and completing the double by beating Bradford 26-10 in the final of the Reserves League Knock-Out Cup. Star riders for the reserves were Ben Howe and Savalas Clouting, who also acquitted himself well in the first team on the few occasions he stood in for injured riders. Clouting scored a maximum in both legs of the Knock-Out Cup final. Other individual performances for Ipswich that year included Rickardsson and Tesar once again reaching the World Final, Shane Parker reaching the World Long Track final at his first attempt and David Norris qualifying for the World Under-21 Final, where he came sixth.

Ipswich were raring to go for 1993. A new racing formula was introduced which meant that teams would be using eight riders instead of seven. This was good news for Ipswich as they were spoilt for choice from their juniors. With the side largely unchanged from 1992 as well as any one from Savalas Clouting, Shaun Tacey, Laurence Hare and the sixteen-year-old local grass track junior star, Leigh Lanham, to choose from, the title looked like a real possibility for the Foxhall Heath outfit. But then it all went downhill. First of all, Tony Olsson was recalled to his parent´track, Exeter, followed by David Norris returning to Eastbourne, where his career had started. Then news came through from Australia that in the very last race of the very last meeting before he was due to return to England, Shane Parker had suffered a severe injury to his foot and could be out for the season. From a championship challenging team, Ipswich now looked as though they could be amongst the strugglers.

Then came the good news. The Ipswich management moved quickly and were able to sign up New Zealander, Mitch Shirra, on loan from Swindon. Eastbourne's season was due to start late and it was agreed that Norris could stay with the Witches for a while. When Belle Vue were defeated by 70 points to 38 in the second meeting of the season, with Dave Norris scoring 14, optimism returned to Foxhall. It did not last long as first Coventry and then Wolverhampton inflicted home defeats on them, although there were encouraging signs in the form of Shaun Tacey and Savalas Clouting. These losses were followed by further home defeats at the hands of Cradley and Arena Essex, and Ipswich sank to the bottom of the table. The latter match not only sent them to the bottom, but it was also the match in which Sam Tesar broke his leg and was ruled out for the rest of the season.

Ipswich never recovered from these setbacks and it was mainly the outstanding form of the reserves which kept the team going. 'The young lads kept us afloat, no doubt about that,' was how John Louis summed it up. In fact they were going so well that Eastbourne even offered £15,000 for Clouting, a bid that was rejected out of hand. In the end, the team finished in eighth place in the league, losing seven matches at home, and was knocked out in the first round of the Knock-Out Cup. Although the season had not lived up to expectations, there were some outstanding individual performances. Both Tony Rickardsson and Chris Louis qualified for the World Final, Rickardsson scoring four points and finishing eleventh,

Left: *A young Ben Howe at the start of his career with Ipswich in 1991. Ipswich have organised Howe's testimonial in 2000.* Right: *Savalas Clouting, another in the long line of young local discoveries, began his career with Ipswich in 1992 and remained in the team until 2000.*

while Louis emulated his father by taking third place after losing in a run-off for second spot against Hans Nielsen. Louis also came third in the Division One Riders' Championship, again after losing in a run-off, this time to Henrik Gustafsson.

Although the juniors were very different in temperament and style, they excelled themselves. The aggressive, determined, gutsy, fast-starting entertainer and showman Shaun Tacey finished the season with an average of 6.62, while the more classically elegant Clouting, who more often than not missed the start but could come through from the back, scored 5.98. The keen, determined, professional, sixteen-year-old Leigh Lanham rode in 17 matches and scored 5.91, which included a 15-point score at Arena Essex. There was a rich vein of local talent waiting to be tapped. It was very reminiscent of the days of John Berry and if it could be harnessed then Ipswich looked set for another golden age.

Ipswich hung on to their outstanding crop of juniors for the 1994 season, but the problem was at the top end, where it was reported at the start of the season that Tony Rickardsson would not be returning, although he actually rode in two matches and scored 20 points. In his place, John Louis and James Easter signed up former Ipswich favourite and world number three, Jeremy Doncaster. Rickardsson he wasn't, but he gave the team a strong third heat leader. Fortunately, the team managed to maintain a very settled look throughout the year, finishing in sixth place in the league. Ben Howe and Savalas Clouting proved to be the pick of the juniors, averaging 6.14 and 5.49 respectively, while Leigh Lanham continued to improve and looked set to emulate his father, Mike, as a Witches favourite. Chris Louis qualified for the World Final again, but could only manage 6 points. Tony Rickardsson won the World Championship, the last to be held under the old one-off meeting style. As Ipswich still held his licence and as he did ride twice for the Witches during the season, it could be said that he was the region's third World Champion (following Ove Fundin and Michael Lee) and Ipswich's first.

Another reorganisation of the leagues for the 1995 season saw the amalgamation of Divisions One and Two into the Premier League. Mitch Shirra was banned for twelve months following an altercation with a referee, but Chris Louis was back and so was Jeremy Doncaster. Local youngsters Ben Howe, Leigh Lanham, Savalas Clouting and sixteen-year-old Scott Nicholls were there to back up the big two. To complete the line-up, Ipswich domiciled Emmerson Fairweather was brought in from King's Lynn. For the Dave Pavitt, John Louis and Mike Western management team it was a dream come true and a return to the John Berry days of using a completely local, home-grown team.

Ipswich were the first track to open in this new era and by the end of June it looked as though the fabulous Berry days were about to be repeated as Ipswich topped the table. In the end injuries put paid to their chances of staying there and they finished in a creditable sixth position out of twenty-one teams. Ben Howe suffered a fractured collarbone on 28 June and soon afterwards Scott Nicholls suffered a nasty concussion riding for Young England. While Howe and Nicholls were out, Ipswich lost three home matches.

Individually, most of the team had their best season ever. Chris Louis showed time and time again during the season that he was England's best rider, finishing with an average of 10.52. This was also the year of the new Grand Prix system for finding the World Champion and Louis finished seventh, though he would have finished higher but for a disastrous final Grand Prix at Hackney. Jeremy Doncaster improved his average from 7.96 to 8.3 and showed

Left: *Tony Rickardsson was world champion three times, twice as an Ipswich rider and once with King's Lynn.* Right: *Chris Louis, now second highest scorer of all time for Ipswich, behind his dad.*

there was still plenty of life in this particular veteran. Ben Howe's average also went up in spite of his long lay-off. Howe had developed into one of the most exciting British riders, noted for his dashes from the back, but perhaps the best performance of all was from young Scott Nicholls. At sixteen years of age, he had a tremendous season, averaging 6.02 and moving ahead of Savalas Clouting in the averages.

As 1996 dawned Witches supporters awoke to the news that their club was in deep trouble. In the middle of January, John Louis stated that he was 'now 99 per cent certain there will be no speedway at Foxhall Stadium this year'. The cause of the problem was the increase in rent, which Dave Pavitt said the company could not afford. Pavitt himself was due to take over at Oxford, leaving Louis and Mike Western in sole charge. It now seemed increasingly likely that Pavitt would take all of Ipswich's assets with him to his new track. Once the threat became known, the town immediately rallied to the club's cause. The MP, Jamie Cann, and the local newspaper, the *Evening Star*, both threw their weight behind the campaign to keep speedway in Ipswich and at an emotive public meeting, attended by around 500 people, £6,000 was pledged in a bid to keep the track open. Louis said that if they could raise £15,000 they would be able to continue. Within 10 days, £17,000 had been raised with local radio station SGR adding a five-figure package to become the team's main sponsors. The team was saved from extinction.

Apart from Emmerson Fairweather, who was replaced by former Witch Kevin Teager, all the riders stayed with the club. Once again Chris Louis was in superb form, confirming his place as top British rider and finishing top of the team's averages with 10.29, which put him into third place overall in the Premier League behind the two Americans Billy Hamill and Greg Hancock. Unfortunately, a last-bend engine failure in the final robbed him of the Premier League Riders' Championship just as he looked certain of victory. Scott Nicholls qualified for the final of the World Under-21 Championship, but was injured just two weeks beforehand, breaking four bones in his left foot. He was told he would be out of speedway for four to six weeks, but he still rode and managed to come fourth despite limping around on crutches. Leigh Lanham also qualified for the Under-21 final, finishing in tenth place, while Savalas Clouting lifted the British Under-21 Championship. Clouting featured in what was undoubtedly the best match of the year, the East Anglia derby against Peterborough, in which he starred in three vital home 5-1 victories in a match full of 3-3 draws. John Louis commented that the crowd for that particular match was enormous and that if they had that sort of support every week, Ipswich would never have financial worries again. Ben Howe continued as the Witches own thrill-maker, continuing to make things difficult for himself, but entertaining the crowd by frequently missing the gate and having to come roaring round from the back. He also increased his average to 7.42. In the end the team finished in eighth place in the league and, given that at one time it looked as though there wouldn't be any speedway at all at Foxhall Heath, most fans were content with that.

The 1997 season saw yet another shake up in the way the leagues operated. Some of the leading teams had felt that the Premier League was too big and that a smaller, more elite league was needed. Ipswich were originally opposed to this move and Mike Western called on the BSPA to retain the old style Premier League for the 1997 season. When it became certain that the new elite league would go ahead, the Ipswich management resolved to let their supporters decide which division they wanted the team to enter – the new creatively titled Elite League or the Premier League, which would become, in effect, a new Second Division. The *Ipswich Evening Star* published a full-page questionnaire and hundreds of supporters wrote in. The majority, which went in favour of entering the Elite League, were probably swayed by the thought of losing both Chris Louis and Scott Nicholls if the Witches dropped down into the Premier League. As it was, Chris Louis pledged his future to the club and was rewarded with a testimonial, while Scott Nicholls withdrew the transfer request he had put in. John Louis soon agreed terms with Jeremy Doncaster and Steve Johnston was signed from Long Eaton. Nevertheless, Louis and Western knew they would have to find a

Car sticker from Ipswich's 1997 season.

world-class rider if they were to succeed in the new Elite League. Ben Howe finally agreed terms, having spent most of the winter, like Scott Nicholls, on the transfer list. The twenty-two-year-old Czech, Toni Svab, was signed to complete the line-up, while Leigh Lanham and Savalas Clouting were loaned out to Premier League clubs.

Without that extra top man, however, things did not go well. In only their third home match of the season, Ipswich lost their unbeaten home run, which stretched back to July 1995, when they had lost 44-46 to Eastbourne. Life was not easy for the Witches in the Elite League, but the turnaround came when the Ipswich management pulled off a major coup and brought former World Champion and former Witch, Tony Rickardsson, back into the line-up in time for the 7 August derby match against King's Lynn. The man to lose his place was Ben Howe, who was loaned out to Poole, but ironically guested for King's Lynn in Rickardsson's first match to give the tie that extra edge. Howe was involved in a heat six incident when he and Scott Nicholls clashed coming off the start line. Nicholls was excluded, then reinstated then excluded again! Ipswich went into an eight-point lead, but were pegged back by Lynn, who took a two-point lead going into the final heat. Louis and Johnston managed a 4-2 to make the final score 45-all after one of the most exciting meeting seen at Foxhall that year. It was also the first time that Ipswich hadn't lost in six matches. The return match at Lynn a week later also ended in a 45-all draw after a dramatic last heat 5-1 from Louis and Rickardsson.

With the arrival of Rickardsson, things picked up and Ipswich climbed the table to finish the season in fourth place out of ten. Rickardsson finished top of the averages with 10.09 from his 10 matches, while Louis was not far behind on 9.42. Scott Nicholls did well in the Elite League, scoring 6.25, while Jeremy Doncaster, the one survivor from the great Ipswich team of the 1980s, once again proved that he wasn't yet over the hill by averaging 6.11.

Individually, Ipswich's riders narrowly missed out on most honours. Rickardsson and Louis finished second and third respectively in the Elite League Riders' Championship, and fourth and ninth in the World Championship. Rickardsson got the consolation prize of becoming Swedish champion for the third time and Louis took the Golden Gauntlet Match Race title from World Champion Billy Hamill in May and successfully defended it five times. Scott Nicholls finished fourth in the World Under-21 Final.

Another new name appeared in 1997 when the Anglian Angels took to the track on 28 March, but there was no new stadium. Instead, Ipswich and King's Lynn had combined their juniors to form a new team to enter the Amateur League. Although they finished bottom of the league, they did make one discovery in sixteen-year-old Matt Read, who finished his first season in league racing top of the Angels' averages with 8.77, scoring 12 points in his debut match against Western Warriors on 28 March. He went on to win the British Schoolboys Senior Grass Track Championship. The only rider to give Read any real support was seventeen-year-old Gary Corbett (also in his first season of competitive league racing) with an average of 8.00. The combined Ipswich and King's Lynn management were not too despondent about finishing last as they saw that the whole purpose of the league was to bring on juniors and they were well pleased with the progress of Read and Corbett.

With the arrival at Ipswich of world number three and top Pole, Tomasz Gollob, the pundits declared that the 1998 Elite League was a forgone conclusion. What other team would be able to stand up to an outfit that included Gollob as well as Rickardsson, Louis and

Nicholls? The pundits were right as the Witches rattled off six successive home victories in their first six matches by scores of 50-39, 54-36, 60-30, 51-39, 61-29 and 53-37. In the same period they also won three away matches. In all, Ipswich started the season with thirteen straight victories and from then on they never looked back, winning the Elite League with the loss of just five matches, as well as the Speedway Star Cup and the Craven Shield. As if the treble wasn't enough, Tony Rickardsson became World Champion for the second time and was ranked at number one in the first ever official World Ranking List, with Gollob third and Louis fourth. Gollob finished third in the World Championship and Louis ninth. The Ipswich Witches had not only totally dominated British speedway but also world speedway. John Louis and Western had at last achieved their ambition of emulating the John Berry era. The other two members of this truly remarkable and unique team that made speedway history were Savalas Clouting and Toni Svab.

It is a sad fact of speedway life that successful teams have to suffer for their success in the following season. Ipswich's combined average in the 1998 all-conquering side was over 46 points. The new rules that came in for the 1999 season meant that Ipswich had to get down to no more than 40 points with a seven-man team. There was nothing for it, two of the leading four of Rickardsson, Louis, Gollob and Nicholls had to go. Nicholls announced he would like to move on anyway to further his career. What came next shocked the whole of the speedway world. The other rider asked to leave was none other than reigning World Champion, Tony Rickardsson, and it was even more of a shock when not only did he go to King's Lynn, but he also took co-promoter Mike Western with him. Toni Svab and Savalas

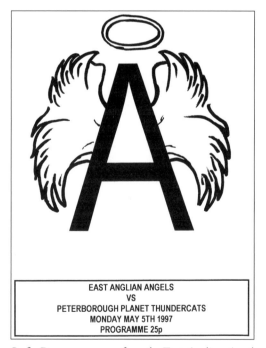

EAST ANGLIAN ANGELS
VS
PETERBOROUGH PLANET THUNDERCATS
MONDAY MAY 5TH 1997
PROGRAMME 25p

Left: *Programme cover from the East Anglian Angels versus Peterborough Planet Thundercats Amateur League match held on 5 May 1997.* Right: *Tomasz Gollob was the world number two in 1999.*

The Ipswich team that swept all before it in 1998. From left to right: Tomasz Gollob, Toni Svab, Tony Rickardsson, Chris Louis, Savalas Clouting, Scott Nicholls.

Clouting stayed, Ben Howe returned, Brett Woodifield came on board from Peterborough and Jason Bunyan was signed up from the Isle of Wight for his first taste of Elite League racing. After a fairly unsuccessful start to the season, Tomas Topinka was released by King's Lynn and John Louis, now joined by his wife Magda as co-promoter, decided Topinka was the man to give the middle order a boost. However, it meant that one of the team would have to be dropped to make way for him. It was a very hard call for Louis to make to Ben Howe, especially as this was the second season in succession he had found himself in this position. As it was, Ben Howe had an average of 6.33 at the time he left and Topinka finished the season with exactly the same average. Apart from one excellent spell in July and August when the Witches won eight matches on the trot, they never looked like the team of old and finished the season in fifth place, which was still good, but not what the Foxhall Heath patrons had come to expect of their team.

Tomasz Gollob took over as number one, finishing the year with an average of 9.24 as well as runner-up in the World Championship. For a long time it looked a though he might actually walk off with the title, but the final Grand Prix round in Denmark came just a week after a horrific crash in which he suffered concussion and lost the tip of a finger. At the time, Gollob was leading the World Championship by four points, having won both the Czech and first Polish rounds, but his injuries proved too much for him and he could only finish the Vojens Grand Prix in ninth place, finally losing out to Tony Rickardsson by thirteen points. Louis' average dropped a little on pervious years as he was dogged by injury and illness. Toni Svab was the greatest revelation of the year as he made the third heat leader spot his own with a much improved average of 7.3.

Five
King's Lynn

Programme cover from 1966, King's Lynn's first full season in the league.

As 1965 dawned, the big news broke that speedway in Norfolk had been saved after all, not at Norwich, but at a town in the north of the county, around forty miles away, called King's Lynn. Maurice Littlechild explained how it happened: 'How did I find King's Lynn? A real slice of coincidence. Jack Thompson and I were nosing around Norwich for an alternative site to house the old "Stars". We thought we had found a beauty near the Royal Showground, twelve acres, four miles north of Norwich. The owner agreed to sell for £4,000 and we'd agreed to co-operate with the Royal Show authorities regarding parking etc. ... A week before the plans were due to be submitted to the council, the owners raised the price to £12,000. A bit naughty. But we went on only to be turned down by the council. Just afterwards, Jack and I, terribly disappointed, were sitting in a tea-room, when the bloke sitting next to us, overhearing our conversation said: "Excuse me interrupting, but why don't you go to King's Lynn. There's an empty stadium there." I investigated and sure enough, there was. It's a little outside the town on the Wisbech Road, between a sugar beet factory and a ... well ... dung factory. All that was there was a chicken farmer, with thousands of flippin' hens running all over the car park! I met the owner, offered a rent and ended up taking a lease to run the dogs and speedway...'

The greyhound track was thirty feet across and the new speedway track was built over half of that. The pits were to be built where the old dog kennels were. Much of the work was carried out by Cyril and David Crane and Olle Nygren. The new promoters went along to the auction being held to sell off the equipment at the old Firs Stadium and bought all the lighting equipment, the body colours, the rakes, the graders and two bikes. The cost was £370.

Before the 1965 season started, however, there was a big shake up in British speedway. For the whole of the previous season, the Provincial League had been operating unofficially. This followed a dispute between the league and the Control Board when the latter, in order to boost the fortunes of the National League, had ordered that the 1963 Provincial League champions, Wolverhampton, should be promoted. Wolverhampton refused, supported by the other Provincial League promoters, so the Control Board outlawed the Provincial League. Unfortunately for the Control Board, the Provincial League continued under its own organisation and managed to run itself very successfully. With the withdrawal of Norwich from the National League, the Control Board realised that something had to be done to reconcile the two leagues and, following a lengthy enquiry undertaken by the High Court judge, Lord Shawcross, it was eventually agreed to end the outlawing of the Provincial League teams and riders and to amalgamate the two leagues into one to be called the British League. Therefore, for 1965, the British League lined up with eighteen teams, but sadly, for the first time since Norwich had entered the Provincial League back in 1937, there was no representative from East Anglia in the official league set-up of the country.

Along with Rayleigh and Ipswich, King's Lynn applied to run on an open licence, with a view to joining the British League in 1966. King's Lynn proved to be the most successful, even though when they opened on 23 May the fencing was still being put up around the track! Maurice Littlechild pulled off a coup by enticing Terry Betts back to the track. Not only did he take part in the first meeting at the new track, the South Lynn Trophy, but he also won it with a maximum that was witnessed by an encouragingly healthy crowd of 6,300. He was offered a contract to ride for King's Lynn the following season. To get him back to match

Left: *Terry Betts won the first ever meeting at King's Lynn, the South Lynn Trophy, with a fifteen-point maximum.* Right: *Cyril Crane's nephew, David, rode for King's Lynn from their first season until 1970.*

fitness, he was loaned out to Long Eaton for the season. In his second match he broke his leg and didn't ride again during 1965!

Fred Rogers attempted a comeback, but after a few outings decided against it. In all, King's Lynn ran a full season of fixtures, challenge matches and individual trophies and, by the end of the season, were ready for their first step into the big time.

During the winter Olle Nygren opened a training school for young riders. The cost was 30 shillings for bike owners and £3 for those wishing to hire a bike. The King's Lynn promoters hoped it would turn up some useful discoveries for the team's league campaign.

With King's Lynn now firmly established, it looked a certainty that league speedway would return to the region in 1966, but it did not turn out to be that simple as King's Lynn's application caused major problems with the number of foreigners allowed into British speedway. The argument between the SRA and the British Speedway Promoters' Association (the BSPA) was particularly silly as King's Lynn themselves didn't want any foreigners in their team, but it caused arguments about whether there should be more foreigners allowed in the league as a whole if it was enlarged by one team. There was also a subsidiary argument about whether Olle Nygren and Arne Pander counted as foreign or naturalised British. Initially, therefore, King's Lynn were only granted an open licence. Eventually, however, common sense prevailed and King's Lynn took their place in the British League, making 1965 the only year between 1937 and 2000 that East Anglia has not had a representative in a major league. King's Lynn's first ever league match was away to Exeter on 29 April, a match they lost by 50 points to 28. They fared a lot better in their first home league match against Glasgow, which they won 45-33, with Peter Moore scoring 12, David Crane 11 and Terry Betts 10.

The Lynn team for that year consisted of Terry Betts, David Crane, former Ipswich favourite Peter Moore, Stan Stevens, Howdy Byford, Ken Adams and Cyril Crane with Alan Jay, Alan Smith, Ray Day, Doug Dearden, Vic Lonsdale and John Mills also making a number of appearances. Betts seemed to show no reaction to what was in effect a two year lay-off and a broken leg, as he carried on from where he had left off with Norwich, becoming Lynn's top scorer with 374 points from 36 matches. Peter Moore also had a good season, scoring 349 from 34 matches, including nine full maximums.

Although King's Lynn finished well down the table in sixteenth position, there was no doubt they had had a successful season. Crowds were well up and the team was beginning to come together. The highlight of the season was when Halifax, eventual league champions, came to visit Saddlebow Road with fifteen straight wins to their credit and the Stars beat them. It was a fitting end to the season.

King's Lynn continued to carry East Anglia's baton alone in 1967. In theory, the team was strengthened by the inclusion of Clive Featherby and Howard Cole and the improvement of David Crane. Unfortunately, injuries played a big part in the season and King's Lynn were the only team in the whole league not to have at least one ever-present rider through the campaign. Peter Moore was injured before the season even started, came back and promptly broke his wrist. When he recovered he got an urgent recall to Australia due to his wife's illness and went home. David Crane and Howdy Byford both missed matches through injury and, at one time, Maurice Littlechild asked to be allowed to sign Ove Fundin, but he was given the thumbs down and Fundin went to Belle Vue instead. Terry Betts continued his wining ways and finished the season with an average of 9.74, but he could not carry the team alone. The loss of Peter Moore in particular was a severe blow and the team finished at the bottom of the league.

With the arrival of Malcolm Simmons in 1968, the Stars were hoping for better things, but although he soon showed his worth and Terry Betts continued his winning form, the team as a whole failed to make much headway. They lost every single away match and finished just one place higher in the league, eighteenth out of nineteen.

In complete contrast to their previous campaigns (1967 in particular), King's Lynn managed to track the same seven riders in every single match in 1969 except one. The septet were Terry Betts, Malcolm Simmons, Howard Cole, Clive Featherby, Allan Brown, Alan Bellham and Pete Bradshaw – who was the only rider to miss a match, the first one of the season, when Geoff Penniket rode before his transfer to Cradley Heath. The result of this was a much more settled side and a rise up the table to ninth place. Betts continued his outstanding form with an average of 9.35. Simmons was not quite as prolific as the year before but nevertheless continued to give excellent support. Howard Cole, as third heat leader, reached the World Final. Both Betts and Simmons won the Silver Sash during the year. They also came first and second in the Southern Riders' Championship, while Betts represented England in the Test match series against New Zealand.

The King's Lynn training school was turning up so many young prospects that it was decided to enter a second team in the Second Division called the Starlets. Unfortunately, they had a disaster of a season, finishing up with more points scored against them at home than

Left: *Howard Cole rode for King's Lynn from 1968 to 1972 and reached the World Championship final in 1969.* Right: *Malcolm Simmons, the world number two in 1976, rode for King's Lynn from 1968 to 1974, again in 1986 and even rode in two matches in 1993, having been co-promoter from 1987 to 1989.*

they got themselves. They used no fewer than twenty-seven different riders as well as four guests and finished bottom of the league with just 8 wins out of 30 matches. The one good thing to come out of the season was the form of youngster Ian Turner, who topped the averages and looked set for bigger things.

The 1970 season saw King's Lynn continue with a fairly settled team. Pete Bradshaw left to go to West Ham and in his place the Stars promoted Ian Turner from their second team. Betts was once again top man, with most maximums, most points, top average, least unplaced rides and easily the most wins, but Howard Cole continued to improve, ousting Malcolm Simmons from the number two spot. He finished the season with an average of 8.49 and took the Silver Sash from Arnold Haley of Sheffield. The middle order was not quite as strong as the year before, with the result that the team dropped three places in the League to twelfth place.

After some misgivings, King's Lynn entered their Starlets once again in Division Two, but midway through the season they transferred lock, stock and barrel to Boston. Ian Turner turned in another good performance, ending the year with an average of 9.35, and a new discovery was made in Arthur Price, who finished second to Turner.

It was a story of much the same again for King's Lynn in 1971. Betts and Simmons managed to improve on their 1970 performances while Howard Cole, plagued by kidney trouble during the season, was still able to better an eight-point average. However, they received little support from the rest of the team. Ian Turner became exclusively a Division One rider for the first time in his career and was just running into form when an injury in August put him out for the rest of the season and Arthur Price was signed up from Boston and showed promise but not much more. Once again it seemed that King's Lynn had the talent but not the results, finishing thirteenth in the league.

As good as Ipswich were, in terms of league placings, they had to play second fiddle to their East Anglian rivals, King's Lynn, who at last managed to get it together in 1972 and finish in the position that their talent deserved. Terry Betts once again improved his average, this time to a magnificent 10.51, Howard Cole stayed at just under 9, while Malcolm Simmons also continued as a high-scoring heat leader. The real difference came with the signing of Australian Phil Crump, who came in mid-season to replace the injured Clive Featherby. Featherby's average until his injury was 4.33, but Crump finished the season with 7.3. King's Lynn finished in a highly respectable third.

Betts had his best year so far as an individual, winning the Golden Helmet from Reidar Eide in May and retaining it through six challenges. He became an automatic Test choice for England, partnered Ray Wilson to the World Best Pairs' Championship and was in the Great Britain World Team Cup squad that won the title.

Left: *Ian Turner rose from the ranks of the Starlets to become a heat leader with the Stars. He rode eleven seasons for King's Lynn between 1970 and 1980.* Right: *Always a controversial figure in the sport, Garry Middleton spent an unhappy year with King's Lynn in 1975.*

ALL ROADS LEAD TO **KING'S LYNN**

THIS SUNDAY, MAY 4th at 3 p.m.

THE

TERRY BETTS

TESTIMONIAL

East Anglia and speedway say "thank you"
to one of the most popular riders of all time.

SUNDAY'S 20-HEAT INDIVIDUAL MEETING includes
European Champion PETER COLLINS, RAY WILSON, DAVE JESSUP, MALCOLM
SIMMONS, TONY DAVEY, NIGEL BOOCOCK, PHIL HERNE, BILLY SANDERS,
JIMMY McMILLAN, BOB HUMPHREYS and
THE KING'S LYNN STARS

A GREAT DAY OUT—DON'T MISS IT!

ADMISSION INCLUDES **FREE** PRIZE DRAW

Terry Betts fully deserved his testimonial in 1975. In all he was with King's Lynn from their opening season in 1965 until 1978. He later returned as team manager.

Things were looking good, therefore, as the 1973 season started. Even though Rider Control had taken Howard Cole away, King's Lynn were not too perturbed. They knew Phil Crump could only improve, especially as he was now no longer commuting between Divisions One and Two, and great things were expected of youngsters Ian Turner, Bob Humpreys, Arthur Price and Barry Crowson. With Terry Betts and Malcolm Simmons still leading, King's Lynn had every reason to feel optimistic. The optimism was soon eradicated as, after just one match, Crump trapped his hand when a car he was repairing fell on him and he was unable to hold a speedway bike for the rest of the season. It also soon became apparent that none of the youngsters were going to break out of the good second-string mould (at least not that season), although 'Tiddler' Turner was just beginning to show what he could do when he was again injured in August and it was left once more to the old firm of Betts and Simmons to see the Stars through. Betts was his usual brilliant self, scoring 418 points from 35 matches, but Simmons went one better as he seemed to take on a new lease of life, moving ahead of Betts in the score chart and recording a 10.26 average. This included nine full and two paid maximums and he failed to record double figures on just three occasions. Towards the back end of the season, King's Lynn signed a young up and coming Swedish rider called Richard Hellsen, who managed an average of 4.5 in 4 matches. In spite of all their problems, the Stars still finished third in the League.

In view of what had happened to Rayleigh, there was good news for King's Lynn fans when it was announced in March 1974 that the Saddlebow Road Stadium had been bought by the directors of King's Lynn speedway. Cyril Crane announced that this meant they could now 'really start planning for the future'.

With the continuing absence of Phil Crump, manager Alan Littlechild was again hoping that his youngsters would at last come good. He knew he could rely on Betts and Simmons, but what he wanted to see was the leap to heat leader status from a least one out of Ian Turner, Barry Crowson, Bob Humphreys or new signing, Ray Bales, son of the former Yarmouth and Norwich favourite Billy, but it was not to be. True, they formed a good solid middle order, but it left the Stars short of that vital third heat leader. Betts and Simmons were once again superb, though Simmons was slightly down on the previous year's scores and Betts regained his spot as King's Lynn's number one. For the first time, Betts reached the World Final, coming tenth with 6 points.

When Malcolm Simmons left at the end of 1974, King's Lynn looked everywhere for a suitable replacement. When Bob Humphreys and Barry Crowson also left, they had to find two more riders. They scoured the length and breadth of the country and came up with Trevor Hedge, Garry Middleton and Olle Nygren, but none of them proved to be really what they were looking for. In the end they looked a little nearer home and brought in the sixteen-year-old school leaver, Michael Lee, and gave him a chance instead. In his first season, Lee became the third heat leader, scoring 182 points from 27 matches, including 1 full and 2 paid maximums. Lee's maximum against Hackney made him the youngest rider ever to score a maximum in the British League. In the end it was just as well King's Lynn had Lee up their sleeves as Betts did not score in quite his usual prolific manner, dropping down to 8.87 points per match. The team finished twelfth out of eighteen, but with Michael Lee in their side they were hoping for much better things in 1976.

As it happened, King's Lynn had very much of a standstill year the following season, finishing in fourteenth place. Their story of the year was that of Michael Lee, who finished the season with a 9.22 average, scoring 8 full maximums in the process. This was a phenomenal record for a seventeen year old in only his second season of competitive racing and first full season in the British League. Comparisons were made with the young John Louis and the feeling was that he might turn out to be even better. In spite of this young wonder boy in their midst, King's Lynn's top scorer was once again Terry Betts, who qualified for the British League Riders' Championship for the tenth year in succession, a feat unsurpassed in the competition's history. With Lee's precociousness and Betts' experience, King's Lynn could have hit the heights if only they'd had a solid third heat leader, but poor Ian Turner suffered from mechanical trouble after switching to the new Weslake and only managed a single maximum all season, finishing with an average of 7.68. Sweden's Richard Hellsen rejoined the stars from White City and showed promise of better things to come.

It was the same old story in 1977, with two top-class heat leaders in Betts and Lee, good second strings, but no third heat leader. In spite if this, King's Lynn did manage to move up the table to sixth place and went one better than the previous year in the Knock-Out Cup by beating Reading in one of the closest finals ever fought, to take the trophy by 79 points to 77. The first leg had resulted in a narrow victory for Reading by 40 points to 38. Back at Saddlebow Road the atmosphere was electric as the two teams fought out another closely run battle. With one heat to go, Reading needed a 5-1 to force a run-off. In the last race, Reading tracked the undefeated Dave Jessup and number two man John Davis, while the Stars had

Left: *Programme cover for the meeting held to celebrate King's Lynn's 500th meeting on 31 March 1979.* Right: *Michael Lee became the youngest ever British Champion when he won the title in 1977 at the age of eighteen.*

Michael Lee, who had been troubled by engine problems all night, and Ian Turner. For three and three-quarter laps, Jessup and Davis managed to hold off the King's Lynn pair, but Lee would not give up and as they came off the very last bend he found some extra speed from somewhere and, in a sensational drive for the line, powered past Davis on the run in. There was pandemonium in the 10,000 strong crowd as the pent-up nervous energy exploded and the realisation struck home that the Stars had won their first ever major national trophy.

For Terry Betts it was his twelfth successive season in King's Lynn colours, in which he passed the 400-match mark and once more averaged over 9 points a match. Once again, though, it was teenage prodigy Michael Lee who stole the headlines. He won his first full England cap, scoring 44 points in 5 matches against the Rest of the World and helped England to victory in the World Team Cup final. He became the youngest ever British Champion and finished fourth in the World Championship final with 12 points. For King's Lynn he easily outscored Terry Betts for the first time, recording an average of 11.16 at home and 10.19 away. All this and he was still only eighteen.

King's Lynn only managed thirteenth place in the league in 1978. As usual, the top two were there to lead the team. Michael Lee, still amazingly only a teenager, top scored with a 10.39 average, and was virtually unbeatable at home while Terry Betts was still good enough to be picked for the England World Team Cup squad. Ian Turner was still the third heat leader, but behind him others were now pushing for that spot; David Gagen turned in a 6.09 average and the Swede Richard Hellsen, improving all the time, did even better with 6.21. During the season, King's Lynn did a swap with Hackney, bringing in the twenty-one-year-old Swede, Bent Rasmussen, in exchange for Billy Spiers. King's Lynn's one triumph in 1978 was to lift the Inter-League Knock-Out Cup. Michael Lee once again became British Champion, finished seventh in the World Final, represented his country in the World Team Cup and appeared in four Test matches against Australasia.

General manager Martin Rogers was able to announce in the winter that he was intending to bring world number four, Dave Jessup, to Saddlebow Road from Reading for a fee of £20,000 in 1979. However, King's Lynn's hopes of at last getting that third heat leader evaporated when, just as Dave Jessup was arriving, Terry Betts decided that fourteen years with one club was long enough and left, first of all announcing his retirement and then changing his mind and going to Reading. Jessup joined new skipper Michael Lee to form the familiar two-pronged spearhead. Nevertheless, by the end of the season that elusive third heat leader had appeared in the form of Richard Hellsen, who finished the season with an 8.58 average. The result of these changes was that King's Lynn shot up the table, finishing fourth and once again reaching the final of the Inter-League Knock-Out Cup, on this occasion losing to Cradley. Off the track, the team was having problems, with the first hint of what was to become a real problem for King's Lynn in the future. Michael Lee was fined £1,000 for failing to turn up at Sheffield for the Inter League Four Team Tournament. He promptly

Left: Programme cover for the 1980 World Championship final, which was held in Ullevi. It was won by Michael Lee with Dave Jessup second and Billy Sanders third. Right: The badge made to commemorate Michael Lee's World Championship victory in 1980.

tabled a transfer request, though this was later 'frozen' when the fine was withdrawn. The season ended on a sour note as Martin Rogers left following a fall-out with promoters Cyril Crane and Alan Littlechild.

Michael Lee had his best World Championship year so far as he grabbed a place on the rostrum, finishing third. Jessup also made the final, finishing eighth with 8 points. Both also represented England in the World Team Cup, but the team failed to reach the final.

In 1980 East Anglian speedway literally ruled the world. On a slick track in Gothenberg on 5 September, during an evening when overtaking proved difficult, Michael Lee at last lived up to his potential and won the World Championship. In three out of his five races, Lee had to come from the back to earn his points – and he didn't overtake just anybody. Two of the riders he passed were former World Champion, Peter Collins, and future World Champion, Bruce Penhall. It was a truly magnificent performance from Lee, who showed what real speedway was all about by keeping a cool head and diving under his opponents as they all in turn moved out wide. But that wasn't all; his King's Lynn team-mate Dave Jessup followed him home in second place and to complete a memorable evening for the region, Billy Sanders of Ipswich came in third. Never since the days of London's pre-eminence on the speedway scene had one area of the country been so dominant in the World Championship. On their way to the final, Sanders had already won the Australian Final and the Australasian Final, while Jessup had won the British Final, in which Lee had come second, and the Commonwealth Final in which yet another East Anglian rider, John Louis, had come second.

And yet it could have been so different for Michael Lee as he started the season in hospital with a serious back injury and had to fight his way back to health. While he was doing this, Dave Jessup was carrying all before him, recording 12 full and 1 paid maximum for the Stars, finishing with an average of 10.52. Michael Lee's recovery enabled him to weigh in with 9 full and 3 paid maximums, but he could only take second place to Jessup in the score sheet with a 10.17 average. The good news for King's Lynn was that they at last seemed to have beaten the handicap they had lived with for so many years in only having two heat leaders. Richard Hellsen had developed into an undoubted star and that third heat leader King's Lynn had desperately sought for so long. Newcomer Mel Taylor, the subject of such controversy between Mildenhall and Ipswich the year before, proved to be a more than useful acquisition as, in his first year in senior league racing, he qualified for the Commonwealth Final and finished the season with a 6.46 average. There was good support too from Bent Rasmussen, who scored 7.49 at home, although he couldn't seem to get to grips with away tracks. Unfortunately, the team stopped there and, in spite of having the World numbers one and two, the Stars dropped two places in the league to finish sixth.

For the third time in three years, the Stars reached the final of the Inter-League Cup and managed to lift the trophy for the second time, beating Swindon 83-73 in the final. King's Lynn were destined to become the last winners of the cup as it was superseded by the Speedway Star Cup from 1981.

King's Lynn started the 1981 season full of optimism. They now had their three top-class heat leaders, none better than their first two, Michael Lee and Dave Jessup. They even had one of the best number fours in the country in Melvyn Taylor. Surely this was going to be King's Lynn's year. Sure enough the Stars started well, a run of ten matches without defeat early in the season looked to point the way to big things. On 4 June, however, came a 34-

Michael Lee at his best in full-throttle action.

point defeat at the hands of Ipswich followed by a home defeat by Coventry. By the end of the season things had got so bad that even Eastbourne managed to gain their one and only away win of the season at Saddlebow Road.

What had gone wrong? The problems with Michael Lee didn't help. He managed to get himself suspended by the club at one time after missing a number of meetings and was stripped of the Motorcycle News Golden Helmet Match-Race Championship after failing to take part in the second leg of his defence against Gordon Kennett at Eastbourne. Off the track he made court appearances in connection with motoring and drugs offences and finally he asked for a transfer. The teenage genius had become the flawed genius and in the year when, as World Champion, he should have been an inspiration to the rest of the team, he had quite the opposite effect and his season-long problems proved extremely damaging to team morale. Ironically, in spite of all his troubles, he was still scoring as though nothing had happened, finishing with an average of 10.34, but he did miss six league matches. Richard Hellsen missed eight matches through commitments abroad, which also didn't help, and no one gave any real support to the top four. David Gagen had the next highest average with 4.88, but even he could only manage to ride in just half of King's Lynn's league matches. Only Dave Jessup and Mel Taylor really came out of this disastrous season that had promised so much with any credit, and the Stars final position of fourteenth out of sixteen just about summed it all up.

As it happened both Lee and Jessup reached the World Championship final again. This time Lee only managed to score 5 points and came tenth, while Jessup came eighth with 7 points. Jessup also represented England in the final of the World Team Cup, helping the team to the runners-up spot behind Denmark.

King's Lynn had another dreadful season in 1982, despite signing up Billy Sanders as second heat leader to replace the Wimbledon-bound Dave Jessup. Top man Michael Lee managed just thirty-five matches for the Stars, while Mel Taylor was the only ever-present member of the side.

Over the close season, King's Lynn witnessed a change of management as former general manager, Martin Rogers, took over the helm as promoter. After leaving King's Lynn at the end of the 1979 season, Rogers had moved to Leicester as promoter, where he was named Promoter of the Year in his first season. When Cyril Crane and Violet Littlechild announced that they wished to lease the stadium and sell the promotion rights, Rogers decided on a move back to what he considered his speedway home. Some people felt this might be a risky move for the thirty-eight-year-old former journalist, but he was very optimistic about the future: 'While many other sports are becoming dated and losing their impact,' he said, 'speedway remains an exciting fast-moving spectacle with a healthy atmosphere … The first priority will be to get together a side which can restore the confidence of the supporters. This has been rather dented in the last year or two … The supporters at King's Lynn won't expect overnight miracles, they are too sensible for that. But fans are the same anywhere. They are genuine people who want to see the sport prosper, and they will always respond to a promoter and riders who are obviously prepared to have a go.'

Bent Rasmussen rode for King's Lynn from 1978 to 1980.

Rogers now set about strengthening the club. His first thought was that he did not want Michael Lee around any more. He felt he was not projecting the right image, nor was he contributing anything to team spirit. Lee was released and went to Poole, while Billy Sanders went back to Ipswich. To take their places, Rogers signed up John Louis, who had requested a move back to East Anglia from Halifax to be near his Ipswich home, and former world number two, Gordon Kennett, from Eastbourne for £15,000. With Richard Hellsen still looking good as the third heat leader and Colin Richardson continuing to improve, better things were hoped for from the season. Six of the team were ever-present through the season, with Richardson missing just two matches. This was in complete contrast to 1982, when King's Lynn had managed to get through seventeen riders during the campaign. Between them, the new promoter, the new signings and the settled team did manage to improve the Stars' fortunes and they finished in a respectable eighth place in the middle of the table.

Rogers major move for 1984 was to sign up old favourite, Dave Jessup, in place of Gordon Kennett. Although Louis, Jessup and Hellsen did not score particularly highly as heat leaders, they were given firm support by the three second strings, Steve Regeling, Kevin Jolly and Martin Dixon. The net result of this solid team performance – five of the them scoring maximums during the year – was that King's Lynn continued their climb up the table to finish in sixth place and reach the semi-finals of the Knock-Out Cup, where they lost to Ipswich.

If 1985 was an unforgettable season for Ipswich, for King's Lynn it was a nightmare. They finished bottom of the league with just five wins to their name, bottom of the League Cup with even less wins and were put out of the Knock-Out Cup in the first round.

The season had started promisingly. Martin Rogers had signed up two good prospects in Paul Woods and Mark Courtney, Dave Jessup and Richard Hellsen were still there and big improvements were expected from Steve Regeling and Kevin Jolly. However, it didn't turn out the way it was expected and by the end of April the Stars had won just one match out of nine. It was then that Rogers pulled off his biggest coup and brought Michael Lee back to Saddlebow Road. Lee's one-year ban for an incident at King's Lynn while riding for Poole ended in May and back he came to his first home, scoring 10 points in his first match. The optimism, not to mention the crowds (up 30 per cent on the previous year), returned as King's Lynn set about making up for lost time. Lee rode in two more matches before declaring that he needed to take time off to look after his business. He returned in June and started off his, and King's Lynn's, British League campaign with a maximum against Wolverhampton in a match that the Stars won by 41 points to 37. Full of hope, the Stars travelled to Oxford for their first away match of the campaign but, unfortunately, Lee didn't. Nor did he turn up for King's Lynn's next home match. Rogers told the supporters: 'This is the last time I am prepared to stand at the gate of a stadium, peering down the road in the hope that Michael Lee will turn up, knowing in my heart that he probably won't.'

Lee asked to be given one more opportunity and even made arrangements to move house from Poole to East Anglia. Rogers, not without misgivings, agreed. Lee returned for the match against Ipswich and, although he only scored 5 points from 5 outings, in his next 4 matches he returned scores of 12, 8, 11 and 12. Perhaps things weren't so bad after all. They might not have been had Jessup not pulled out of the match against Reading, complaining about the track. For this action, Jessup was fined £500 and given a six month ban, suspended

Left: *Dave Jessup had two spells for King's Lynn, from 1979 to 1981 and 1984 to 1985. Jessup was desperately unlucky not to win the 1978 World Championship when a push-rod snapped while he was comfortably in front in his first ride. He went on to score 11 points, while champion Ole Olsen finished on 13.* Right: *Richard Hellsen, a King's Lynn regular from 1979 to 1985.*

for two years, for 'foul and dangerous riding, disorderly and ungentlemanly conduct and conduct prejudicial to the sport'. It was Jessup, however, who saved the Stars from the ultimate humiliation, when two second places at Sheffield prevented King's Lynn from being whitewashed. Lee had turned up for the match without any machinery. He then failed to turn up himself for the match against Ipswich and for Richard Hellsen's testimonial. Rogers suspended him indefinitely and placed him on the transfer list. At the end of this total disaster of a season, Rogers put the business up for sale, but no one wanted it and Rogers agreed to carry on, signing a three-year deal with the stadium's owners. The only bright spot for the 1985 season was that King's Lynn Juniors won the British League Junior Championship with a team that included Jamie Habbin, the British League Junior Riders' Champion.

King's Lynn fared no better in 1986 than they had in 1985. They managed the remarkable feat of losing all ten home matches, though they did manage to win two away. It left them ten points adrift at the foot of the table. During the season, the Stars used nineteen different riders – no less than fourteen of them new to King's Lynn colours. The major new signings at the beginning of the season were American captain, Bobby Schwarz, and Belle Vue's Andy Campbell on loan. Michael Lee was given yet another chance, but after he failed to turn up for a match at Sheffield in June he was suspended for a month and set in train a chain of

117

events that was to see him out of speedway until the beginning of 1991. Other new signings included Einar Kylingstad and Stephen Davies, while Malcolm Simmons also made a welcome return to Saddlebow Road for ten matches. Only Schwarz lived up to expectations and far too often he had to carry the team. He finished the season with a 9.06 average. For the third year running, King's Lynn were destined to finish at the foot of the table, but at least they managed to win four matches at home, even if they did lose the lot away.

The big signing of 1987 proved to be Richard Knight. Signed just as the season was about to start, Knight took some time to get going, but once he did he easily outscored the rest of the team, finishing up with an average of 8.35.

In spite of three years of poor results, the crowds at Saddlebow Road had held up well. As Martin Rogers put it: 'Whilst people in King's Lynn, including me, are keen to see the team improve its status and get a few more results, I think what has kept them coming is that it's acknowledged as a good speedway, and we try very hard to create the right environment for good competition.'

Rogers finally managed to sell the track to Bill Barker and former King's Lynn star, Malcolm Simmons. Their first signing was yet another American, Lance King, from Cradley. He was followed by twenty-year-old Dane, Allan Johansen, who was left without a club after Hackney had decided to drop into the National League. The third signing was John Davis from Reading. All three were on loan from their parent clubs. Finally, just as the 1988 season

Left: *By 1985, Michael Lee's mercurial career was almost over, although he did continue to appear on and off for King's Lynn until 1991.* Right: *American captain, Bobby Schwartz, more or less carried King's Lynn in 1986.*

The 1987 King's Lynn team. From left to right, back row: Einar Kyllingstad, Andy Campbell, Stephen Davies, Steve Regeling. Front row: Ray Morton, Richard Knight (captain, on bike), Mick Poole.

was about to start, Bo Petersen was lured out of retirement. With these new signings, together with Richard Knight and Stephen Davies, it looked at last as if King's Lynn had a team worthy of the British League and one that would not come bottom. Nevertheless, for some reason, the team did not seem to click and the crowds began to drift away. Simmons felt that a number of the team were not pulling their weight and said so. Bo Petersen, in particular, was thought to be riding so far below what he was being paid that the management offered him a revised pay deal, which he refused and took himself off to Wolverhampton. Although King's Lynn rallied in the middle of the season, with four wins out of four in July, they finished it as they began by winning just three matches out of twelve during the last two months. In the end, though, they did get out of the cellar position for the first time in four years, finishing one place above Ipswich.

With the run of poor results and the falling crowds, Simmons began to talk seriously about dropping down into the National League for the 1989 season: 'I'm looking at a cheaper way to run and, in my opinion, a better way to run as well. If people want to see King's Lynn in the British League it will cost them £5 a head to get in. But, if they just want to see speedway, they can see National League racing for £3.50. The only difference between the two leagues is half a dozen world-class riders.'

Individually, Lance King topped the averages, scoring 7.75 per match, followed by John Davis on 7.69, with Richard Knight, the Stars only ever-present that season, as third heat leader on 7.45. John Davis qualified for the World Championship final, scoring 3 points and coming twelfth. Though in a well-publicised exchange with England managers, Eric Boocock and Colin Pratt, this was not enough to get him into the international team.

King's Lynn opted to stay in the British League for 1989 after all, but Malcolm Simmons didn't. He resigned, leaving Bill Barker in sole charge. The season started with a settled squad that contained Richard Knight, Lance King, John Davis, Allan Johansen, Stephen Davies, Adrian Stevens and the late 1988 season signing, Armando del Chiele, who all came back for the 1989 season. Dave Jessup was signed up as team manager and for once everything at Saddlebow Road looked rosy.

It just wasn't King's Lynn's luck to have everything go well for a change. Del Chiele had been scheduled to make five trips back to Italy during the year, in the end he made about a dozen and, in all, missed seventeen matches. Stephen Davies got caught up in World Team Cup meetings in Australia and got injured. John Davis left for Swindon, following an argument about his contract, and in the end King's Lynn finished in their accustomed position at the foot of the league, making it four times in five years. For good measure they got knocked out of the Knock-Out Cup in round one.

There were some bright spots in King's Lynn's 1990 campaign, such as the form of new signing, Mark Loram, who, in his British League debut season, went straight to the top of the averages and the late season signing of world number six, Henrik Gustafsson. In addition, the Speedway Control Board decided to allow former World Champion and Stars number one, Michael Lee, to take up his racing career in King's Lynn colours, following a petition from 400 supporters and letters from other British League promoters arguing that a return by Lee would be good for speedway in general and good for the league in particular. Richard Knight qualified for the World Championship final and scored 7 points to finish in tenth position. These pieces of good news were not enough to stop the team finishing bottom yet again for the fifth time in six seasons. They won just six home matches and during the whole season only one rider managed a maximum – Richard Knight, who scored 14 paid 15 against Belle Vue on 17 June.

Before the 1991 season began Bill Barker revealed the club was losing money hand over fist and their continued existence was very much in doubt. Mark Loram, Bo Brhel and Henka Gustafsson spearheaded their assault on the league along with Denis Lofqvist. Team boss, old Stars' favourite Terry Betts, picked Bo Brhel as the difference between the team finishing in bottom spot and their final reasonably respectable eighth out of thirteen final placing, thus ending their dismal run of last places.

The Commonwealth Final was held at Saddlebow Road in 1991, a meeting that was to prove yet another landmark on the rocky road of former teenage prodigy, World Champion and wayward genius Michael Lee as Barker managed to persuade him to act as supplementary reserve for the meeting. The decision to answer Barker's call was a decision Lee was to regret as he was called into replace the injured Craig Boyce in heat nineteen. He finished last but was subsequently chosen for a random drug test, which he failed to take. He was suspended pending a hearing. At the hearing he explained that because he was only a reserve he had stopped on the way to the meeting for a drink and did not take the test in case the alcohol showed up. It was one step too far for the authorities who banned him from racing.

Left: *Richard Knight, who rode for King's Lynn from 1987 to 1994, qualified for the World Championship final in 1990.* Right: *Henka Gustafsson appeared for King's Lynn from 1990 until 1993 and finished fourth in the 1992 World Championship.*

Bill Barker had high hopes for 1992 at King's Lynn. He had got together a team that could take on the best in the League. Brhel, Gustafsson, Loram and Lofqvist were still there and in had come Alun Rossiter and New Zealand champion Gary Allan, with Lynn junior Darren Spicer at reserve. Hopes were raised even higher when Rossiter scored 11 points in his first meeting and King's Lynn then beat Ipswich at Foxhall Heath.

Everything went well until the end of May. The Commonwealth Final, which had proved so fateful the year before, was to prove ill-omened yet again. A 4,000 strong crowd turned up and Barker removed the £26,000 takings to the safety of his Kent home. It did not prove very safe as all the money was stolen. Barker called a crisis meeting at the club to explain to the supporters just how precarious the Stars' position now was. Crowds were down eighteen per cent and this latest blow was almost enough to finish King's Lynn off. A fighting fund was set up and nearly £6,000 was raised by the fans, but it was nowhere near enough. After a home defeat to Belle Vue and then, suffering the worst possible luck, the next two meetings being rained off, Barker announced in mid-July that his company had gone broke and was no longer trading. Speedway devotees in East Anglia were devastated. They had just witnessed the return to the fold of Mildenhall for 1992, who had then promptly gone out of business. Surely, King's Lynn was not going to go the same way?

The 1992 King's Lynn team. From left to right, back row: Alan Littlechild (manager), Darren Spicer, Gary Allan, Henrik Gustafsson, Bo Brhel, Bill Barker (co-promoter). Front row: Dennis Lofqvist, Mark Loram (captain, on bike), Alun Rossiter.

It was former rider Keith 'Buster' Chapman who came to the club's rescue. Following a somewhat clandestine meeting with the league's management committee at Arena Essex, he became the new promoter. After the announcement that he was to take over, Chapman said 'I'm still seeing the psychiatrist!' He then proceeded to introduce himself to King's Lynn supporters by riding a couple of laps of the Saddlebow Road circuit dressed as Mickey Mouse. There was nothing Mickey Mouse about the situation he faced or the measures he needed to take to make the team solvent and ensure continued racing in Norfolk. Within a month of his arrival, King's Lynn had managed to complete just one Saturday fixture in twelve weeks, hardly ideal for a Saturday racetrack.

Chapman's first attempt at putting the track back on an even keel was to increase admission prices and renegotiate the riders' contracts. In the end, all but one of the riders – Alun Rossiter – stayed. Kevin Brice was brought in to fill the gap. Chapman then postponed the scheduled league match with Reading because his two star riders, Mark Loram and Henka Gustafsson had commitments abroad. He was promptly fined £1,000 by the BSPA and Reading were awarded the match 75 points to nil. Chapman refused to pay the fine and in the end it was suspended for two years.

Gradually, events began to turn Lynn's way and they managed to complete their league programme, finishing in ninth position. Gustafsson finished with an average of 8.86 and Loram with 8.85. Dennis Lofqvist took Brhel's place as third heat leader and finished with 7.54. There were other successes too: the reserves finished second in the Reserves' League, with Darren Spicer and Emmerson Fairweather both turning in averages of at least 9 points a match. Mark Loram reached the final of the World Long Track Championship, finishing in fourth place, while Gustafsson reached the final of the World Championship, also finishing in fourth place. There is no doubt, though, that the biggest success was in finishing the season at all. Chapman lost in the region of £20,000 in the short time he was there, but he was ready to try again in 1993. He had found some new sponsors and together with stadium owner and team manger, Alan Littlechild, he was hoping for great things in 1993.

There were many pre-season jitters as, after an initial telephone call from Henka Gustafsson, in which he indicated he would return to King's Lynn in 1993, nothing was heard from him for several months. Bo Brhel, who had also agreed to return, had gone into hospital to undergo an operation on a broken wrist while Dennis Lofqvist couldn't agree terms and asked to be put on the transfer list. Buster Chapman moved to cover possible absences and persuaded Richard Knight to return. He also signed up Saddlebow Road track specialist, Glenn Doyle, from Bradford for a reported £10,000.

There was much relief for Chapman when Brhel arrived in England just before the start of the season. The relief was short-lived, however, as he was on his way back home again within twenty-four hours due to problems with his work permit. Doyle was also a victim of red tape. Just as he was about to march out on the pre-match parade for the opening match

Left: *Jason Gage, King's Lynn, 1992.* Right: *Bo Brhel was a King's Lynn stalwart from 1991 through to 1999, apart from a brief sojourn at Oxford in 1996. Hailing from Zlin in the Czech Republic, he has been Czech national champion three times, in 1992, 1993 and 1998.*

of the season, he was informed he was not allowed to ride for King's Lynn, because his FIM track licence did not contain the words 'British League'. King's Lynn lost their opening match 45-63 to Arena Essex. By the following Saturday everything had been sorted out and Brhel and Doyle both helped the Stars come back from a 12-point deficit to defeat Belle Vue in a 55-53 thriller. Eventually, a month after the season had started, Gustafsson also turned up and took his place in the team, just as Doyle broke his wrist and just before Mark Loram broke his collar bone. With the World Championship semi-final at Ipswich coming up, King's Lynn pleaded with the Control Board to allow Loram to be seeded straight through to the final, but they would not agree and Loram was forced to strap himself up and hope for the best. He managed just one and half laps before the pain proved too much and his assault on the 1993 World Championship was over.

With both Doyle and Loram out, a 'new' rider appeared in King's Lynn colours when the forty-seven-year-old former Star, Malcolm Simmons, turned out for them at Belle Vue, scoring 0 points from 4 outings. He appeared once more, scoring 3 points at home to Coventry, but then packed it in again. Lynn's rider troubles continued as Gustafsson was rushed to hospital suffering from appendicitis and an application for a work permit for Czech rider Tomas Topinka was turned down by the Department of Employment. Chapman appealed against the decision and the DE eventually relented.

With all the problems they were encountering, it was no surprise that by mid-June the Stars were rock bottom of the league but, even worse for the long-term future of Saddlebow Road was the fact that crowds were falling. Only 1,400 turned out to see a star-studded line-up compete for the Barum Trophy. Chapman admitted that the average gate had fallen to 1,350, which was 250 below the break-even figure. By September the rider situation had sorted itself out a little. John Wainwright and Paul Dugard joined the team from Eastbourne, Gustafsson was back from hospital and Brhel found some real form, lowering the track record to 60.1 seconds and then becoming the first man to get below 60 seconds with 59.5. Results began to go King's Lynn's way and they eventually finished the season in ninth out of the eleven teams.

With Loram's attempt on the World Championship over, it was left to Henrik Gustafsson to carry the Stars colours, which he did with his usual determination and skill, reaching the final and scoring 10 points. He was also reserve for the victorious Swedish team in the World Pairs final, scoring 6, paid 7, points from 3 outings and was a member of the third-placed Swedish team in the World Team Cup final. He came second in the Division One Riders' Championship. Tomas Topinka qualified for the World Under-21 Final, scoring 7 points, but was the only man to beat eventual winner, Joe Screen.

When Chapman announced that he had been unable to agree terms with Henrik Gustafsson at the start of the 1994 season, it seemed to be another case of 'here we go again' for the Stars. However, Chapman managed to sign a good replacement in the form of Bobby Ott as well as bringing back Malcolm Simmons as team manger. Chapman's faith in Loram was repaid as he became the world-class rider Chapman knew him capable of becoming. He topped the averages with 9.46, qualified for the World Championship final, where he scored 9 points and finished eighth, and was England's top scorer in the World Team Cup final, scoring 9 points and two bonus points. Tomas Topinka took fourth place in the World Under-21 Championship.

Bobby Ott had a turbulent season for King's Lynn in 1995.

The crowds were still not great and at one time, midway through the season, Chapman declared that he could no longer carry on and he put the club up for sale. However, he was deluged with letters from the fans asking him to stay, so after just two weeks he took King's Lynn off the market and decided to continue. As for the team itself, they did manage to get themselves out of the doldrums, finishing fifth out of eleven in the league.

King's Lynn's 1995 Premier League season got off to a bad start when Bobby Ott lashed out at an Ipswich starting marshal, after finishing third in heat eleven of the match at Foxhall Heath. Referee Graham Brodie fined him the maximum possible £250 and the incident was reported to the Speedway Control Board, whose manager, Graham Reeve, happened to be at the meeting. Ott was subsequently suspended for two meetings. After the relative high spot of fifth place in 1994, King's Lynn returned to their accustomed lowly position, finishing nineteenth out of twenty-one.

One of the most exciting matches of the season at King's Lynn was the final Test match in which Australia clinched the series with a 59-49 win over England. The new lay-down engines were allowed in this match, which resulted in Bo Brhel's two-year-old track record of 59.5 being equalled or lowered six times during the evening: Chris Louis finished up with the new record of 59.2. As lay-down engines were to be allowed in the Premier League in 1996, it looked as though the whole league was in for a spate of new track records.

Having seen the match, Buster Chapman was not convinced about the correctness of the decision to allow lay-down engines. He told the *Speedway Star* that: 'In the days when bikes were slower the racing was just as exciting. The other day I was watching a video of the England *v.* Sweden match from the seventies when Terry Betts and Malcolm Simmons helped England get a memorable win. There was tremendous close action all night, and those bikes were so much slower than today's models … If there was a re-match now, with the top boys out on lay-down bikes, it would be very, very fast, but at the expense of rider skill and judgement.'

Meanwhile, Chapman's message to his supporters at the end of the season was: 'I'm working on getting a strong team together – and if that means running in mid-week then so be it. … We have lost continuity as a team because of key riders being absent through weekend championship and continental engagements. … I want to see the King's Lynn Stars team together, racing together and working together, that way it's good for club morale and the fans have continuity with the race night and the riders they are supporting. I am still thinking hard about the situation, but it really does seem to me that if we want to put a competitive team out then we will have to go for a mid-week date.'

The news at King's Lynn was even worse than at Ipswich going into 1996. Bert Chapman announced in January that he had been unable to agree a new deal with the Littlechild family, who were asking for increased rent. Chapman was concerned that he was being asked to pay more without any improvements being made to the stadium. He said it was not fair on the supporters and that urgent work was needed on the toilets, car parks, floodlights and general appearance of the stadium: 'We have always had top-class racing at King's Lynn on a super track, but without any improvements to the stadium I have to ask why I should pay more rent.' Cyril Crane countered by saying that Alan Littlechild just did not have the necessary finance and that he and the Littlechild family were working hard to put together a consortium to take over the stadium. He went on to say that in his view, 'if the Stars had a successful and winning team they would get support'. To complicate matters even further, the Littlechilds put Saddlebow Road up for sale with an asking price of £500,000. The supporters caught in the middle of all this could only voice their frustration and their spokesman, Neville Lake, said: 'In this situation the supporters are going to be the losers – and as I see it there is nothing they can do.' No agreement was reached in time for the season and the BSPA put Chapman's licence on ice for a year. Cyril Crane and Alan Littlechild proposed running a team in the Conference League, the new name for the Academy League, but the BSPA refused to transfer the licence and, for the first time in thirty-two years, the summer at Saddlebow Road did not reverberate to the roar of speedway machines or emit the smell of dope (methanol). Behind the scenes frantic efforts were being made for a return in 1997 as Chapman realised that the only way he would be able to continue to run speedway at King's Lynn was to buy the stadium himself.

During the 1996 season, Chapman's intention of buying King's Lynn stadium still held and although the deal was delayed by the Littlechild family's control of the stadium going into receivership, he continued to scout round for riders to enter the new Elite League. A new problem arose when it was discovered that the stadium had been badly vandalised and would need somewhere in the region of £100,000 worth of repairs to put it right. Even this did not faze Chapman and he announced he was close to signing up old favourites, Tomas Topinka and Bo Brhel for the 1997 campaign. Ivan Henry joined Chapman as co-promoter and then came the shocks for the King's Lynn faithful. First of all it was announced that race night was to be Wednesday, that the team's colours were to be blue, yellow and silver (green being considered unlucky) and that the team's nickname was to become the Knights, thus ending the long association with the old Norwich Stars.

Shane Parker and Paul Hurry were signed up and everything was almost ready, with just one drawback – Chapman had still not bought the stadium! The good news finally came on 10 March 1997, when it was announced, not only that the stadium had been bought but that the team line-up had been completed with Simon Wigg and Shaun Tacey. On 21 March, the Knights raced their first match away to Peterborough. No one gave the team a chance as they were taking on one of the favourites for the league title, but it was King's Lynn who ran out winners by 49 points to 41.

Although this was all good news for the fans, Chapman now found he had a monumental task on his hands, getting the almost derelict stadium back into action in less than a month. Chapman and his band of volunteers worked all day and all night to get the stadium ready for opening day. Speedway returned to Saddlebow Road on 9 April when the new Knights defeated Eastbourne in a close-run Speedway Star Cup match by 46 points to 44 with Wigg, Parker and Brhel all reaching double figures. By the end of the season, King's Lynn had finished in fifth place, Wigg had reached the final of the Elite League Riders' Championship, where he finished in fourth place, and Brhel had reached the final of the World Long Track Championship, finishing twelfth.

King's Lynn also reached the final of the Craven Shield after defeating Ipswich in the best match of the year. Trailing by ten points after the first leg, the Knights knew they had to pull off a spectacular home victory to progress any further. With one heat to go King's Lynn were fourteen points in front, needing to prevent Ipswich gaining a 5-1 if they were to progress

A former world under-21 champion, Leigh Adams joined King's Lynn midway through the 1999 season and averaged over nine points per match.

into the next round. Most times this might not have been too difficult, but the Ipswich riders for the last heat were Tony Rickardsson and Chris Louis while Simon Wigg and Shane Parker were King's Lynn representatives. In a memorable final race, all four riders diced wheel to wheel for the whole four laps and were four abreast down the straights. At one point on the final lap, Parker briefly nosed in front but was overtaken by Rickardsson. However, Parker did just enough to hang on to second place to prevent a 5-1 and to send King's Lynn through. It was not to be a fairy tale ending though, as they lost to Coventry 107-73 in the final, losing both legs.

Chapman would have liked to have finished the season on a winning note, but he was more than pleased with the way he had turned King's Lynn's fortunes round. Crowds were very low to start with, by mid-season they were good, and by the end of the season they were brilliant. 'I have never had a year like it,' said Chapman. 'With all the hassle I had at the start with the stadium, to have a season like this was outstanding. Everything was good, the team was nice to work with and we had lots of fun.'

For King's Lynn, unlike Ipswich, 1998 was a season best forgotten. Beaten seven times at home and not winning one single away match, this left King's Lynn in ninth position in the league. A team called Norfolk made its appearance during this year, having taken over from Skegness in the Conference League when the latter folded in mid-season. Norfolk was in fact King's Lynn who agreed to provide a temporary refuge for the Skegness outfit. Top rider was Peter Boast, who averaged 8.05. The team finished fourth in the league.

Just before 1998 came to a close, Keith Chapman announced that King's Lynn would be running in the Premier League the following season. He then announced a new management team of Mike Western and Brian Griffin who quickly made their mark by signing World Champion Tony Rickardsson, Stefan Andersson, Martin Dixon and Robbie Kessler to add to old faithfuls Bo Brhel and Tomas Topinka and, sooner than it was possible to believe, King's Lynn were back in the Elite League. Not only that but there was every hope that this year some silverware might find its way onto the Saddlebow Road mantelpiece, but these hopes were quickly dashed as the Knights lost their first eight matches.

The new management team moved quickly to stop the rot and signed former World Under-21 Champion, Leigh Adams, from under Belle Vue's noses. Tomas Topinka was the rider who had to go to make way for him. Although it was too late to save them in the Craven Shield, where they finished in seventh place, Adams' signing did boost their chances in the League itself. Indeed, so it proved, as Adams' average of over 9 points per match helped King's Lynn become one of only three teams to go through the league season unbeaten at home and to finish in third place, equalling their highest ever league placing way back in 1972 and 1973.

In Tony Rickardsson they had the man of the year. Rickardsson repeated his 1998 success and became World Champion for the third time, joining a very select band of riders to do so – Ove Fundin, Barry Briggs, Ivan Mauger, Ole Olsen, Erik Gundersen and Hans Nielsen. Leigh Adams also had a good World Championship, finishing in seventh place overall.

King's Lynn decided to enter a team called the Braves in the Conference League in their own right, following their rescue of Skegness the previous year. It wasn't a great success and they finished bottom, having used a total of twenty-six different riders in just twelve matches, without a single rider managing to take part in all twelve. The major discovery was Australian Darren Groves, who has now moved on to the Premier League with Workington.

Six
Peterborough

Before Peterborough's arrival on the scene, there had been other attempts to run speedway in Cambridgeshire, as this advertisement from the 8 October 1938 edition of Speedway News *shows. Wisbech, in fact, ran amateur speedway from 1938 to 1939 and again from 1946 to 1948.*

There were stories during 1964 that a new track was to open at Peterborough. Former Yarmouth rider, Ivor Brown, was said to be ready to open the track towards the end of the season on an open licence as a precursor to entering the Provincial League in 1965.

Towards the end of 1965, there were more stories in the press about a new track opening at Peterborough. This time the man behind the venture was said to be Ron Wilson. The track received planning permission from the council on 26 November and made an application to run in the British League. In the end, however, Peterborough's bid to enter the world of speedway came to nothing as further planning difficulties eventually prevented the plans from reaching fruition and the application had to be withdrawn.

Peterborough finally made it for real in 1970 as they at last resolved their problems with the council and declared they would be ready to open in mid-May. The new promoter was Danny Dunton, on behalf of Allied Presentations, who said they were ready to lay out £10,000 on the provision of a track, safety fence, lighting, pit area and speedway offices at the East of England Showground Stadium, Alwalton, just outside Peterborough. The Panthers' first match was an away fixture, a Knock-Out Cup match against Rayleigh, which they lost by 48 points to 30 on 11 April.

Most of the team put together by Danny Dunton were either fairly new to speedway or had been around for a while without setting the speedway world alight and not much was

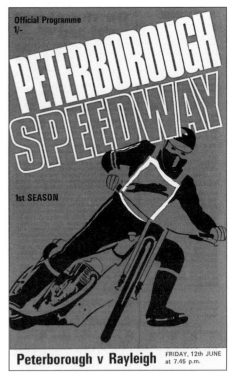

Left: *Brian Clark made his debut for Peterborough in 1970 and continued riding for the Panthers until 1979. He is currently the club's third highest scorer of all time.* Right: *Programme cover for Peterborough's first ever meeting on 12 June 1970.*

Roy Carter first appeared for Peterborough in 1971 and stayed until 1977.

expected from them in their first season. There were, however, a number of surprises in store for the critics. Top scorer, Andy Ross, turned in a useful 9.08 average and was ably backed by Richard Greer with 7.49 and Peter Seaton with 7.14. Peterborough finished the season in tenth place, a very respectable showing for their first year.

For 1971, Peterborough were looking to improve on their mid-table initial season performance. Andy Ross was in good form, Roy Carter was signed from Long Eaton and Pete Seaton was expected to become the third heat leader. However, Seaton broke a thumb before the season even started, Ross broke his leg after just eight matches and Carter proved to be very inconsistent, which left Richard Greer to more or less carry the team on his own and the Panthers finished up one from bottom of the league. The only bright spot was the form of sixteen-year-old John Davis who was loaned to Peterborough from Oxford towards the end of the season.

There was a decided upturn in Peterborough's fortunes in 1972 as the team finished in third place, thanks to an outstanding year from Richard Greer. They also finished runners-up to Crewe in the Speedway Express Cup, losing in the final by 67 points to 89. Support for Greer came from John Davis, who upped his average by over two points per match, and from Roy Carter and former Ipswich riders Clive Noy and Ted Howgego. When the Panthers captured John Harrhy on loan from Coventry, it really looked as though they would win the title. However, Harrhy was recalled after only nine matches and then John Davis broke his collarbone, Ted Howgego did likewise and Clive Noy broke his leg. In spite of all this

Peterborough still managed third spot. No less than three of the team held the Silver Sash at some point in the season: Greer won it twice, Davis managed three successful defences and Carter four.

The Panthers continued to enjoy success at the top end of the table in 1973, even though they dropped a place to fourth. Top man was Richard Greer with 8.96, while at the bottom end was Jack Walker with 5.72, a difference of just 3.24 between best and worst. The one big improvement came from Brian Clark, who upped his average by over two points to 7.28. He also won the Silver Helmet.

Peterborough, now East Anglia's only representatives in the Second Division, started the 1974 season in deep trouble as both their numbers one and two, Richard Greer and John Davis, opted to ride in the First Division. Just before the season started the team's number three, Frank Smith, was recalled to his parent club, Coventry. Fortunately, they were able to obtain the services of Mike Lanham from Birmingham, though he too eventually returned to his parent club, Ipswich, but not before racking up 337 points in 35 matches. With a vastly improved Brian Clark, however, it was enough to keep Peterborough's head above water and they managed to finish in the top half of the table, eighth out of nineteen.

Peterborough started off their 1975 campaign with six straight losses, including two matches at home, and things didn't get much better. Brian Clark tried extremely hard and finished with a nine-point average, but he had no real backing and the Panthers finished eighteenth.

Peterborough unearthed a promising teenager in 1976, two in fact, but after scoring four and seven in his first two matches Paul Tapp decided that speedway was too expensive and packed it in. The other was Ian Clark, who had just started to show great promise when a broken leg put an end to his season. If he'd have continued in the side, Peterborough may well have improved on their final ninth position. Brian Clark was again top man at Alwalton, followed by Tony Featherstone. As with King's Lynn though, Peterborough's main problem was the lack of a consistent third heat leader. There was a sound middle order with the likes of Roy Carter, Steve Taylor, Ken Matthews and Kevin Hawkins, but it was that extra bit of sparkle up top they needed. Perhaps Ian Clark would provide it when he returned next year.

Peterborough's eighth season finally brought them their first honour – on 7 August 1977 they won the National League Four Team Championship on their own track. This success spurred them on to a much better league campaign than the previous three years and they finished up fifth. As expected, Ian Clark started the season as a regular team member, but with Roy Carter and Steve Taylor both leaving the team, there was a vacancy for the final place. Team manager Ron Orchard had two possible replacements in twenty-one-year-old Peter Spink and Nigel Flatman, who was on loan from Ipswich. He hit on the idea of using a double header programme to decide who would get the last place. In the first match against Crayford, Flatman scored 6, paid 8 from 3 rides. He was riding so well in fact that he was brought into the team in place of Ian Clark for the second match against Scunthorpe, where he scored a paid 6 from 2 starts. Peter Spink was given his chance and he scored a paid 11 from 4 starts, which left Mr Orchard with something of a headache, deciding to whom the last team place should go. In the end Nigel Flatman was given the nod and finished up his first season with an average of 7.16. Ian Clark's performance continued to improve as he

Ian Clark appeared for Peterborough from 1975 to 1979 and again in 1985.

finished with 7.57, but Andy Hines proved himself to be the Panthers' best rider with an average of 7.97.

Peterborough registered another fine year in 1978, finishing sixth overall. Dave Gooderham, the former Ipswich junior, arrived and became an immediate hit, topping the Panthers' averages at the end of the season, Andy Hines was second, while Ian Clark took the third heat leader spot, just ahead of Nigel Flatman, Kevin Hawkins and Brian Clark. But, considering Clark's average was 6.31, it shows what a solid look Peterborough had to their team. Not only that, but when given his chance late in the season, teenager Tim Hunt also recorded an average of 7.33 from 11 matches. Brian Clark missed one meeting during the year, the first he had missed for three seasons.

Because of the wealth of junior talent available in East Anglia, 1978 saw the introduction of a new league, The Trackstar Anglia Junior League, which was the brainchild of Peterborough team manager, Ron Orchard, and sponsored by the Peterborough-based speedway accessories company, Trackstar. Each team was to consist of three riders who would race over three heats in the second half of their parent track's meetings. Payment was to be at the rate of 50p per point. The idea was to encourage junior talent by giving them experience in match conditions on various tracks and to give them a taste of riding in front of big crowds. To make sure the league was kept for juniors only, riders became ineligible once they had completed six British and/or National League matches. Ten teams made up the league: Ipswich, King's Lynn, Peterborough, Mildenhall, Crayford, Boston, Hackney, Rye House, Cradley Heath and Leicester. The league was won by Ipswich, who lost just two matches out of eighteen. Top rider for Ipswich was Andy Hibbs, Craig Featherby topped King's Lynn's scorechart while Richard Knight was Mildenhall's third best with an average of 7.33. For Peterborough, Ian Barney rode in 6 matches, scoring 13 points. In an inter-league match at the end of the season, the Anglia League beat their Scottish counterparts by six points.

The major event of Peterborough's 1979 season was the announcement of Brian Clark's retirement. Clark had been with the club since they first entered league racing in 1970 and had ridden in 330 league and cup matches, scoring well over 2,000 points at an average of around 7 points a match. It was only fitting that the promoters, Danny and Lee Dunton, should offer him the post of team manager on his retirement. In this, his final year, Clark still managed an average of 7.24 at home and an overall average of 5.77. Strangely enough, just as Clark was calling it a day, another of the Panthers original 1970 team, Richard Greer, was making a welcome return to his old track. His average of 7.50 made him second heat leader behind the much improved Nigel Flatman, an ever-present in the team but whose continued improvement ironically made it more and more certain that he would be reclaimed by his parent club Ipswich for the 1980 season. The team finished eighth in the league, two places down from the previous year, while Nigel Flatman finished runner-up in the Junior Championship of Great Britain.

The 1980 season was a standstill year for Peterborough as they once again finished in eighth position. Nigel Flatman was overtaken as Peterborough's number one by Andy Hines.

Nigel Flatman in action for Peterborough in 1977. Flatman turned out for the Panthers from 1977 to 1980 and again from 1986 to 1987. He had one final period from 1989 to 1990.

Peterborough 'Skoda Panthers' body colours.

The experienced Richard Greer claimed the third heat leader spot and also took on the role as trainer in chief for the young riders.

Peterborough's main achievement in 1981 was in beating British League Halifax in the first round of the Speedway Star Knock-Out Cup, but then it was on their home track, which was to prove typical of the Panthers season: almost unbeatable at home, unable to win away. This fact was reflected in the averages of top two Andy Hines (10.00 at home and 6.37 away) and Richard Greer (9.7 at home and 6.36 away). Unsurprisingly, this inconsistent form left them in the middle of the table, ninth out of nineteen. The Hines brothers, Andy and Mick, were both ever-presents for Peterborough, as were the other two Andys, Buck and Fisher.

Peterborough were still unable to win matches away from home in 1982, but unfortunately they also lost four at home and did not prove to be nearly as unbeatable as they had the previous season. Dave Allen and Andy Buck continued to improve and the Hines brothers, as usual, showed 100 per cent commitment to the club, but the Panthers could not make up for the loss of Richard Greer, who left the Showground at the end of 1981. In the end they finished a poor thirteenth in the league and were knocked out in round three of the National League Knock-Out Cup. Andy Hines did make a good showing in the National League Riders' Championship to finish fourth.

Nigel Couzens, who rode for Peterborough between 1976 and 1981.

Peterborough had a new number one for 1983 in the shape of Ashley Pullen, who was signed up from Oxford in the close season to take the place of Andy Hines, but once again it was a very mediocre season for the Panthers. They rose just one place in the table to twelfth and got knocked out of the cup in the second round by neighbours Mildenhall.

Peterborough's run of poor performances managed to get even worse in 1984 as they finished just three points above bottom team Edinburgh. Apart from Derek Harrison, who only rode in six matches, top of the averages was Mick Hines with just 7.5 from his 33 matches. With this score, he wouldn't even have been a heat leader in Long Eaton's championship team of that year! Amazingly, Peterborough provided the winner of the National League Riders' Championship when Ian Barney beat Dave Perks in a run-off for the title at Peterborough on 13 October. The first attempt at staging the final at Wimbledon had been rained off after eight heats, at which stage Ian Barney had scored no points!

In 1985 Martin Rogers decided to chance his arm in the National League, taking over Peterborough from Danny Dunton. To get them out of the doldrums, Rogers decided on a policy of selling and buying to bring the team up to strength. What he hadn't reckoned on, however, was the fact that speedway in Britain was going through one of its periodic down phases during the winter of 1984/85. Poole, Exeter, Eastbourne, Newcastle and Wimbledon all pulled out of the British League, leaving a lot of new riders available for the National League and, in the process, upping the standard. For Rogers, it meant he found it more difficult to sell or exchange the riders he had wanted to dispose of. However, he was able to bring back two former Panthers' favourites in Ian Clark and Kevin Hawkins, move Keith Bloxsome in from his other track, King's Lynn, and divert new Australian arrival, Mick Poole, from Saddlebow Road to the Showground. He also brought in former Panther, Ken Matthews, as team manager. In the end he was able to dispense with the services of Mick Hines, Keith Millard and Neil Cotton, and so the team had a distinctly new look about it.

The first major piece of good news came on 30 June when Peterborough beat Mildenhall at West Row 41-36. It was the first time the Panthers had brought back two points from an away fixture since September 1981, almost four years before. Something had to be going right!

In the end Peterborough finished seventh in the league, a rise of seven places. Kevin Hawkins revelled in his return to the Showground, topping the averages with 9.12 and coming second in the National League Riders' Championship, while Mick Poole slotted straight in as second heat leader with 7.52. Dave Allen, one of the few survivors from 1984, was third with 7.27.

One curious statistic (it can't be called a match!) occurred at the end of the season when, on 4 October, Peterborough registered an all time speedway record, defeating Birmingham by 65-0 after Birmingham had refused to ride on a rain soaked track.

Peterborough maintained their solid middle of the table look in 1986, finishing in tenth position. Kevin Hawkins was once again top man, just above Nigel Flatman, who returned to Alwalton after six years. Newcomer Carl Baldwin transferred from Mildenhall and took over the third heat leader spot.

Peterborough continued their climb up the National League table in 1987, finishing in fifth place. Their away record of three away wins was their best since 1980. One of the major reasons why Peterborough were at last turning into title challengers was the form of Ian

Neil Cotton, seen here in Rye House colours, rode for Peterborough in 1982.

Barney. For four years he had averaged around the 6-point mark. In 1987 he suddenly came good and shot to the top of the Panthers' score sheet with an average of 9.16. With Kevin Hawkins, he reached the final of the Best Pairs, where they came second to Mildenhall. Hawkins continued to score well for Peterborough, while Nigel Flatman kept up his performance as third heat leader.

Peterborough continued their middle-of-the-road existence in 1988, coming eighth. The main news was that David Hawkins took over as promoter from Martin Rogers midway through the season. The top three in the team were new signing Mick Poole, and the ever-dependable Ian Barney and Kevin Hawkins.

The following year was to prove to be another standstill season for Peterborough, as they finished eleventh in the League. Kevin Jolly came in for Kevin Hawkins and the top three of Mick Poole, Jolly and Peter Chapman all scored over 8 points per match, while Ian Barney dropped down to 7.27. Nigel Flatman returned to the fold after a season away, but once again it was all middle-of-the-road stuff. The one high point was the victory for the Panthers in the National League Four-Team Tournament.

Like Ipswich, Peterborough also started 1990 well, winning five out of their first seven matches. Mick Poole raced in three of those matches and scored 40 points. Then, at about

Left: *Ken Matthews rode for Peterborough from 1973 until 1977 and returned for 1979. He was brought back by Martin Rogers in 1985 to act as team manager.* Right: *Kevin Hawkins first rode for Peterborough between 1976 and 1978, and returned in 1986 to have three more seasons with the club. Appointed team manager in 1992, his inspirational leadership led the Panthers to the Second Division treble from wooden-spoonists the year before.*

Left: *Jason Crump, the only Peterborough rider to be part of both the 1992 and 1999 treble winning sides.* Right: *Stephen Davies was the only survivor of the bottom place 1991 team to make it into the 1992 championship winning team.*

twenty past eight on Wednesday 30 May, Poole came a cropper while trying to overtake Rod Hunter in heat six of the match at Long Eaton. He smashed into the fence and was taken off to hospital with a broken thigh. After that, Peterborough were never the same team again. Ian Barney left for Exeter shortly afterwards and the Panthers finished up in their customary mid-table position in tenth place. Mick Poole returned to top the averages with 9.58, with Craig Hodgson in second place. Newcomer, Frank Andersen, took the third heat leader spot.

Behind the scenes, team spirit was not all it might be. Paul Blackbird asked for a move to Milton Keynes, Frank Andersen found it hard to settle and left before the end of the season while Craig Hodgson's outspoken nature did not endear him to promoter David Hawkins, who referred to it as an 'attitude problem'. There were also question marks over the financial viability of the club and its long-term future. All in all a season to forget for Peterborough, but who knows what might have been had not Mick Poole made a split-second miscalculation at twenty past eight on a spring night in Long Eaton?

If 1991 was a difficult year financially for King's Lynn it was an even worse one for Peterborough, whose promoters finished up the season going in to liquidation and whose team finished up the season in bottom place of the British League Division Two. The future looked very bleak for Peterborough, but their rescue was just around the corner: 'Peterborough are back on the speedway map again and heaven help the other clubs!' This was said by James Easter at a public meeting as he announced that, with Peter Oakes, he had taken over the Panthers in time for the 1992 season after former promoter David Hawkins had had his licence suspended. With ex-Peterborough favourites, Kevin Hawkins, appointed as team manager, Richard Greer as clerk of the course and Ken Matthews as junior team manager, the new promoters set about building a team to challenge for the title. Their first signing was Ade Hoole on loan from Wolverhampton, but he never appeared. After going back to the drawing board, six times World Champion, Ivan Mauger, was taken on as overseas scout and one of the greatest Czech riders of all time, Vaclav Verner, as coach. There was more success with the signing of Mark Blackbird from Long Eaton and £9,000 was paid for Paul Whittaker, though he was soon to be replaced by Nevill Tatum. Mick Poole returned after a year's absence in the First Division and the sixteen-year-old Jason Crump, son of former world number three Phil Crump, also signed on the dotted line. Paul Hurry came on loan from Arena Essex and Rod Colquhoun was next, which left just one place for a member of the 1991 squad, that being Stephen Davies.

The opening match resulted in a 49-41 victory over the Swedish touring side, Rospiggarna. Poole, looking like he had never been away, top scored with 14 points, while Crump made a sensational debut, scoring paid 11 from 4 rides. From then on, apart from one or two minor defeats, there was no stopping the Panthers, who went on to win the Second Division, the HEAT Team Championship and the Knock-Out Cup. They became only the second team in Division Two history to go from wooden-spoonists to champions in successive seasons. It was particularly remarkable that Peterborough's success occurred without any of the team making it into the top fifteen averages in the league. This just served to show the all-round strength and balance James Easter and Peter Oakes had put together and also what an inspirational team manager Kevin Hawkins turned out to be. Mick Poole topped the team's averages with 8.77, followed by Jason Crump, in his first ever season, on 8.4. It was a remarkable turnaround for Peterborough. As the *Speedway Star* headlined it in their Track Review of Peterborough the team went 'From Rags to Riches'.

Having been given the option of promotion, Peterborough decided to stay in the Second Division for financial reasons. The championship winning side of the previous year broke up before the 1993 season started, with Alan Davies refusing to accept the new BSPA pay rates and then making any further discussion over pay futile by injuring himself in the Australian Championship final. Neville Tatum also decided the new pay rates were not for him and Jason Crump moved to Swindon. Alan Mogridge arrived from Arena Essex and was appointed captain, while Eric Monaghan was taken on after the demise of his own team, Stoke.

In spite of all the changes, Peterborough performed well and, although they did not manage to retain their title, they did finish in a very respectable third spot, thereby establishing themselves as one of the leading teams in the division. As usual, the Panthers were very strong at home, winning all of their twenty matches. Mick Poole was particularly formidable at home, averaging 10.44. He also achieved the runners-up position in the Division Two Riders' Championship after losing a run-off for first place against Swindon's Gary Allan. Alan Mogridge and Eric Monaghan provided solid backing as the second and third heat leaders while newcomer Jason Gage, signed up from the ill-fated 1992 Mildenhall team, performed well, averaging 6.51 as Peterborough's number seven.

Left: *Mark Blackbird, another member of the 1992 treble winning Panthers.* Right: *Ryan Sullivan joined Peterborough in 1994 and stayed with them through to their triumphant 1999 season, apart from 1998, when the team dropped into the Premier League.*

Peterborough's top two riders of 1993, Mick Poole and Alan Mogridge, both left at the end of the season, as did Paul Hurry. In came Australian Ryan Sullivan, Carl Stonehewer from Belle Vue and former world finalist and Ipswich rider, Zdenek (Sam) Tesar. The net result of these changes was that not one of the 1992 championship winning team remained just two years later!

More changes occurred during the season as firstly Ian Barney, the club coach, gave way to his own protégé, Scott Nicholls, and then late in the season the forty-year-old Alan Grahame came in for Jason Gage, who admitted that he was no longer enjoying his speedway. Grahame rode in 6 matches for the Panthers, averaging 9.29. Thirty-year-old Sam Tesar was enjoying a new lease of life after fracturing a leg while riding for Ipswich. He got better and better as the season went on and, apart from Grahame, finished as the Panthers' top rider with an average of 9.13. At the other end of the age scale, nineteen-year-old Ryan Sullivan was amazingly the Panthers' only ever-present rider. It was amazing because he had arrived from Australia just after injuring an elbow and then sustained a shoulder injury. In spite of these injuries he looked an exciting prospect. With a neat, clean-cut style of racing, he averaged 7.09 in his debut season and looked a good bet for an exciting future in the sport.

In the end the Panthers finished in fifth place in the league and, although they won six matches away, unusually for them they also lost five at home. One of the reasons for this was the fact that they were a completely new team and many of the opposing riders had had more experience of the Showground than the home team had!

Peterborough were the only Second Division team not to sign up a First Division rider as the two leagues amalgamated for the 1995 season. They also became the first former Division Two team to defeat a former Division One team in the new Premier League when they beat King's Lynn in April. Peterborough were hoping for big things from Ryan Sullivan and they got them. Finishing the season on 8.86 as well as winning the overseas title, he became the Panthers' number one, just ahead of Sam Tesar on 8.38. With the return of Mick Poole from Oxford, Peterborough had a trio of heat leaders capable of mixing it with the very best in the Premier League, which is exactly what they did. They finished the season in fourth place and were runners-up in the Four Team Tournament. This was a truly remarkable effort that was helped once again by the return of the unbeatable home performance. In complete contrast to Ipswich, however, not only did Peterborough not have any local riders in the team, they did not even have one British rider in the team. The rest of the team was Hans Clausen, Jens Rasmussen, Ronni Pedersen and Marian Jirout.

Peterborough were in no rush to change their successful 1995 side, but changes were forced on them as first Mick Poole announced his retirement and then Jens Rasmussen did likewise. At the end of January, the Panthers' management stunned the speedway world by signing up World Under-21 Champion, Jason Crump, for a record £35,000. Crump had, of course, begun his racing career as a sixteen-year old at Alwalton in 1992 and now he was welcomed back with open arms. With strong backing from an ever-improving Ryan Sullivan and the reliable skipper, Sam Tesar, the Panthers enjoyed their best season since winning the Division Two title back in 1992, the same year Crump had ridden for them before. They finished as runners-up in all three major competitions – the Premier League, the Speedway Star Cup and the Four Team Tournament. As well as all their team runners-up prizes, Jason Crump also finished runner-up in the Premier League Riders' Championship.

This was to be Kevin Hawkins last year as Peterborough team manager. He had begun his riding career back in 1976 with the Panthers and made more than 250 appearances for them. He had moved on to Coventry where he had six good years in the British League before returning to Peterborough to play a major part in the amazing transformation from the bleak days of 1991 to the position where the Panthers were now one of British speedway's leading clubs.

As one of the top teams in the country now, it was only natural that the Panthers should opt for the Elite League. The top four from the successful 1996 team – Jason Crump, Ryan Sullivan, Sam Tesar and Mario Jirout – all agreed to stay on. Jan Staechmann was signed up, as was Rene Masden, and everything looked set for a useful 1997 campaign. However, right from the start it all seemed to go wrong. In their opening home fixture, the Panthers lost their unbeaten home record, which had stretched back to 1994, to King's Lynn. It was becoming apparent that while Crump and Sullivan and to a lesser extent Tesar were pulling in the points, the rest of the team was struggling. The team was boosted when Kelvin Tatum was brought in to replace Staechmann, scoring a maximum in his second match, but although Tatum provided much needed support to Crump and Sullivan, Tesar's form unaccountably disappeared and for most of the season he was left struggling. The Panthers finished the inaugural Elite League in ninth place out of ten, although their strength at heat leader level did

Sam Tesar also started riding for Peterborough in 1994 and stayed until 1999.

mean they were able to win the Four Team Tournament, with Crump scoring a maximum in the final. Crump finished the season fourth in the Elite League averages with a 9.71 average.

After a very poor season financially as well as in the league, Peterborough opted to drop down into the Premier League for 1998. This meant a complete change for the team, with Glenn Cunningham, Brett Woodifield, Nigel Sadler and Jan Andersen being signed up, while the last three places went to juniors, David Howe, Oliver Allen and Simon Stead, who were members of the successful 1997 championship winning Peterborough Amateur League side. With Kevin Hawkins taking over the role of youth development director, Peterborough embarked on a policy of encouraging young riders and, in an unprecedented display of strength at junior level, entered a record number of ten riders for the 1998 British Under-21 Championship. This was an astonishing turnaround for a team that just three seasons ago had not tracked a single British rider.

The new team got off to a dream start by winning their first eight matches. Glenn Cunningham in particular was most impressive, averaging 10.8 over the run. Of the juniors, David Howe looked the most likely to succeed and finished the season with an average of 7.7, in spite of a broken wrist. Cunningham finished with an average of 9.68 as well as winning the Premier League Riders' Championship. All of this meant that Peterborough won the Premier League Championship at their first attempt as well as the Premier League Fours and the Premier League Pairs.

David Howe was a member of Conference League champions Mildenhall in 1997, a member of Premier League champions Peterborough in 1998 and a member of Elite League champions Peterborough in 1999.

If Rickardsson was man of the year in 1999, then Peterborough were team of the year. Jim Lynch wanted to take his Premier League winning side into the Elite League, but Peter Oakes disagreed and left. Ian Jarvis joined Lynch and together set about building a team fit for the top division. Back came Jason Crump, Ryan Sullivan and Sam Tesar, who had all been out on loan during the Panthers' year in the Premier League, as well as Mario Jirout. They were joined by Nigel Sadler and David Howe from the 1998 team in addition to Jan Andersen, who was on loan from Edinburgh. It looked a good enough team, but even the promoters weren't really prepared for what lay in store. The Panthers swept the board, just as Ipswich had the year before, taking the Craven Shield, the league title and the Speedway Star Cup. Jason Crump's form was nothing short of phenomenal, as he topped the Elite League averages by well over half a point and won the Elite League Riders' Championship. He also finished eighth in the World Championship and won the Golden Helmet in September from top British rider Mark Loram, defended it successfully four times and finished the season as holder. He received strong support from Ryan Sullivan, who finished third in the overall Elite League averages and tenth in the World Championship. Nigel Sadler and David Howe both did well in their first season of Elite League racing, averaging 5.97 and 5.53 respectively. Sadler came third in the World Under-21 Championship, while Howe finished the year having been part of a winning team in every one of his three seasons in speedway, winning the Conference, Premier and Elite League titles in three successive seasons. No wonder he is much in demand!

Seven
Mildenhall

Programme cover from Mildenhall's first ever meeting on 18 May 1975.

At the back end of 1974 came the news that a new track would be operating in Suffolk. Farmer Terry Waters had provided the site in April 1973 for promoter Bernie Klatt to carve out a training track. By November 1974, Mildenhall boasted a 300 yard circuit constructed on a 1,000 ton chalk base with a red shale surface. Open meetings were being held and the hope was that a team would be ready to enter the British League Division Two in the 1975 season.

Some local residents objected to the track, citing noise as a reason. The local Public Health Inspector arrived with his sound equipment just as a bomber was landing at the nearby American airbase. He didn't even bother to take any soundings of the noise coming from four speedway bikes!

One youngster who could be seen practising on the track during 1974 was Michael Lee, the fifteen-year-old son of scrambles star, Andy. Michael, who was due to leave school at Easter 1975, hoped to go straight into speedway and already had a future lined up with King's Lynn. 'Dad's not too keen on the idea,' Michael was reported as saying, 'he'd prefer that I concentrated on scrambling, I think. He says there's more money to be made, but speedway has a special attraction for me.' The *Speedway Star* felt that Michael Lee could be a name to watch for the future.

On 18 May 1975, Mildenhall were able to welcome Scunthorpe for their first home match of the New National League (as Division Two had been renamed) campaign. The team for that first match was Bob Coles, the captain and said to be 'the rock on which Mildenhall was founded', Fred Mills, Stan Stevens, Roger Austin, Alan Witt and Graham Kerr with Kevin Jolly at reserve. It was not an auspicious start as the Fen Tigers lost by 37 points to 41. They lost the next eight matches too. Mildenhall were to find it hard going all season, but gradually the team

Three stalwarts of Mildenhall's early years. From left to right: Kevin Jolly, Rob Henry, Mel Taylor.

came together. A few signings were made, including veteran Chris Julian on loan from Exeter, and things didn't look so bad. In the end the Tigers finished one from bottom, nineteenth out of twenty, but the important thing was that they had arrived and were to give East Anglia another team to shout for.

Mildenhall's first announcer was Terry Ripo, who had had experience of announcing at Rayleigh and Hackney. He was rung up by Mildenhall's front man, Colin Barber, before the start of the season and asked if he would like to give it a go on a six-week trial. Twelve years later he was still there, but he says that no one ever told him if the six-week trial was successful or not! His announcer's box was originally mounted on six upended railway sleepers. If the crowd got excited they could move the box and make it shake. Alan Cowland once kicked the door in after disagreeing with a refereeing decision. Fortunately for Terry he was on holiday at the time of this incident, but when he returned he found a big hole in the door to his box.

Like Ipswich, Mildenhall hoped to find their own riders from their own training school. In 1976, four more trainees from their winter school – Fred Mills, Robert Henry, Mick Bates and Neil Leeks – joined the team on a more or less regular basis. The slightly more experienced Mills was the pick of the bunch, but promoters Colin Barber and Bernie Klatt had high hopes for all of them. Until they could rely on a team of home-grown talent, Mildenhall used some more experienced riders. Bob Coles topped the averages with 9.1 and in the middle order Alan Cowland and Stan Stevens contributed 6 and 5 points respectively. Another local training school product, Kevin Jolly, came on so fast (averaging 8.63 per match) that he was reclaimed by his parent club Ipswich, who sent Trevor Jones in exchange. Jones too thrived in the Mildenhall atmosphere and finished with an average of 7.88.

The 1976 season was a year of consolidation for the newly formed Fen Tigers as they rose four places in the table to finish thirteenth.

Mildenhall also improved their league position in 1977, finishing in eighth position under the expert captaincy of Bob Coles. The Fen Tigers continued to unearth more home-grown talent at their training track. This time it was sixteen-year-old Mel Taylor, who was unlucky not to score a maximum in his first season when his exhaust came adrift. As it was he finished the season with a home average of 7.08 from 8 matches. Robert Henry continued to improve and Mildenhall felt they were now reaching the stage when they had lost that old training track tag and were being taken seriously as a team ready and able to challenge for league honours.

Mildenhall's progress could not be sustained in 1978 and the team dropped to twelfth place. The season started badly when Trevor Jones, plagued with a wrist injury, announced his retirement from the sport. Fens Tigers' promoter, Colin Barber, moved quickly to sign up a replacement and persuaded Leicester to loan them Ray Bales.

Mildenhall almost provided the sensation of the season when, in the Inter-League Cup, they lost by just one point to the reigning British League champions, White City. It could even have been a victory but for a dubious decision when the referee excluded Robert Henry following a collision between Henry and Gordon Kennett. The White City rider later admitted that the incident was his fault.

A mid-season row between Mildenhall and Ipswich stirred up much controversy in the region. It all began when Mildenhall loaned Mel Taylor to Reading part of the way through the season. John Berry complained that Mildenhall had given their word that when they felt Taylor was ready for British League racing, Ipswich would be given first refusal. Mildenhall

Trevor Jones leads for the Fen Tigers as they take on Weymouth, with Neal Leeks sandwiched between Weymouth's Malcolm Corradine and Chris Robbins.

countered by saying that they had given Ipswich permission to approach Taylor earlier in the season but that no approach had been made. Following further accusations and counter accusations the relationship between the two clubs slumped to an all-time low, with the result that all Ipswich riders were banned from using the training facilities at West Row.

The biggest blow to the Mildenhall team came when Bob Coles announced his retirement in August. At the time he had an average of 8.04 and was third to Ray Bales and Mel Taylor. Mildenhall never really recovered from this blow and they slid down the league.

Of all the East Anglian teams, there is no doubt that 1979 was Mildenhall's year. In little more than five years since the track they were riding on had been a field producing potatoes and carrots, the Fen Tigers became league champions. The Cinderella team of British speedway had arrived. The title was finally won on a chilly November night in Scunthorpe, when the team recorded a 45-32 victory to take the title by just one point from Rye House. Of the seven riders in the team that night, all had been born in East Anglia and no less than five of them had come through Mildenhall's own junior training sessions.

Two close season signings clinched the title for Mildenhall. The first was the return to speedway of the former Yarmouth and Ipswich rider and manager, Ron Bagley, who took over the team management. The second was the transfer of Mick Hines from British League Wimbledon. The first seven home matches saw Mildenhall top the fifty point mark, including two 60-18 thrashings handed out to Scunthorpe and Crayford. The season finished with fourteen victories out of the last sixteen matches. Mildenhall's strength was that every one of their riders was capable of a big score. Richard Knight was the only rider not to score a maximum, though even he scored paid 11 from 4 rides in one match – and it has to be remembered he was still a teenager in only his second year of competitive racing. Three men topped the 9-point average mark: top was Ray Bales with 9.56, followed closely by Mick Hines and Mel Taylor. The rest of the team were Mick Bates, Robert Henry and Mike Spink, with Mark Baldwin putting in 9 appearances.

The team also reached the semi-finals of the National League Knock-Out Cup where they lost to Berwick and Mel Taylor finished third in the Junior Championship of Great Britain. As if all that wasn't enough, they also won the 1979 Trackstar Anglia Junior League, losing just four matches from twenty-two. Mark Baldwin top scored with Mark Bilner just behind. It was a high point on which original consortium member Colin Barber decided to retire.

Mildenhall lost Mick Hines at the start of the 1980 season and replaced him with the Fen Tigers only non-East Anglian, Ian Gledhill. He hailed from the West Riding area of Yorkshire and was transferred from Stoke for £6,000. Unfortunately, Gledhill was unable to settle in at West Row and it became apparent that Mildenhall were going to struggle to keep hold of their league championship. A nineteen-point defeat at lowly Milton Keynes on 1 July was a sure sign that all was not well and so it proved as Mildenhall slipped to seventh place in the League. Ray Bales was the pick of the bunch yet again followed by Robert Henry.

Mildenhall started the 1981 season under manager Bernie Klatt like a team inspired, winning nine of their first ten matches and topping the league in mid-June. They also finished the season with a hat-trick of wins, but in between they only managed eight wins out of twenty-three, including one spell where they were beaten seven times in a row. Looking at the averages at the end of the season it is hard to see why Mildenhall should have lost so many matches. Three riders, Robert Henry, Ray Bales and Ian Gledhill, finished with averages of

Mildenhall's Neal Leeks crashes with Peterborough's Nigel Couzens.

over 8 points per match while two more, Mick Bates and Richard Knight, finished with averages of over 7. Richard Knight in particular was very impressive as the twenty-two-year-old raised his average by another point per match. Although eventually finishing only eighth in the league, the Fen Tigers did enjoy a good cup run, losing in the semi-final to the eventual winners, Edinburgh.

The arrival of Derek Harrison and the continued improvement of Richard Knight injected new life into Mildenhall in 1982 and with the solid scoring of Ray Bales, the Fen Tigers finished the season in second place to Newcastle. It was to be the start of a remarkable run for Mildenhall.

Mildenhall again finished runners-up in the League in 1983 behind Newcastle, just three points adrift. Derek Harrison continued as top man, with the ever-improving Richard Knight as second heat leader. There was solid support from Carl Baldwin, Robert Henry and Carl Blackbird, with newcomer David Jackson and Andy Warne providing good backing. The team lost in the semi-finals of the cup to eventual winners, Exeter, while Richard Knight finished runner-up in the National League Riders' Championship final behind Steve McDermott.

For the first time in Second Division history, a team finished runners-up for the third season in succession when Mildenhall finished just one point behind the champions in 1984. The two Carls, Baldwin and Blackbird, both showed big improvements over their previous performances and Robert Henry was back to his best. Ray Bales returned to take the place of Richard Knight.

Mildenhall suffered their own tragedy in 1985 when, on 30 July, promoter and founder Bernie Klatt committed suicide in a carbon copy of Billy Sanders' suicide. The former chef, who had helped turn a carrot field into a purpose-built speedway track and make Mildenhall

Mel Taylor rode for Mildenhall from 1977 to 1979 and 1986 to 1988, becoming Mildenhall's second highest scorer of all time.

Rob Henry rides round the outside of Glasgow's Charlie McKinna and Andy Reid (1980).

into one of the National League's most successful outfits, had decided to take his own life. He left his widow, Elaine, and brother, Barry, in charge of the team.

Great things had been expected of the Fen Tigers, runners-up three times in succession, and it seemed that this could be their year. They lost Ray Bales at the beginning of the season, but managed to sign former Fen Tiger, Andy Hines, from Ipswich to take his place. At the end of May, Carl Blackbird moved on to Belle Vue for £20,000, later winning the Junior Championship of Great Britain, but Klatt signed up Rob Hollingworth to replace him. Another former Fen Tiger, Mel Taylor, also returned to West Row later in the season, but then Bernie Klatt died and there were problems behind the scenes.

Barry Klatt announced that, with the support of owner Terry Waters, a new consortium including Barry himself and Skid Parish would take over the running of the club. However, Elaine Klatt, who had become the licence holder on the death of her husband, refused the offer from the consortium and a major row erupted. The behind-the-scenes drama affected performances on the track so much that most of the team failed to turn up for their final away fixture at Peterborough and the Panthers were awarded the points. The team dropped to fifteenth place in the league. Apart from Blackbird, who had a 9.64 average at the time of his departure to Belle Vue, the top rider turned out to be Mel Taylor with 7.84, closely followed by Carl Baldwin on 7.82. All in all, though, it was a season Mildenhall wanted to forget.

The legal wrangling at West Row continued throughout the winter, but in the end the new consortium took over in time for the new 1986 season with Skid Parish and general manager Barry Klatt responsible for the day to day running of the team. Their first problem was Kevin

Ian Gledhill (left) and Richard Knight, two of Mildenhall's leading riders from the early 1980s.

Jolly, a £14,000 signing from King's Lynn, who refused to ride after a disagreement about a loan for new equipment and, after just two weeks as a Fen Tiger, was transfer listed. The consortium's biggest coup was in signing former world number two, Dave Jessup, for £12,500 from King's Lynn. During the negotiations, Skid Parish was very impressed with Jessup's keenness, especially when he went out to buy a pair of mudguards in Mildenhall colours even before the negotiations were complete! Jessup inspired the whole team and finished the season with an average of 10.69. Eric Monaghan was also signed from British League club, Odsal, and became number three man. Sandwiched in between was old East Anglian favourite Mel Taylor, who improved his 1985 average of 7.84 to 9.11. Captain Robert Henry also gave good support, recording a 7.04 average.

A major incident occurred during the season when, on 11 June, Mildenhall refused to ride at Long Eaton, claiming the track was unfit. The Speedway Control Board fined the club £1,000 with £1,000 costs. In addition, Robert Henry, Dave Jessup and Mel Taylor were fined £250 each and Eric Monaghan, Rob Parish, Richard Green, Wayne Dunworth and team manager, Maurice Everett, had to pay £200 each. All parties were banned for six months, suspended for two years.

In the end the team managed seventh place in the league and reached the final of the Knock-Out Cup, losing to league champions, Eastbourne, by 90-64 in the final.

For the fourth time in six years, Mildenhall finished runners-up in 1987. Their troubles now behind them, the Fen Tigers were able to concentrate on racing. In a three-horse race for the title between themselves, Eastbourne and Stoke, Mildenhall led the league in September, but fell away just at the wrong time as Eastbourne headed home. Eastbourne also beat

Mildenhall in the final of the Knock-Out Cup. In consolation, as well as the Best Pairs, Mildenhall won the National League Fours.

Melvyn Taylor became a prolific scorer, finishing with an average of 10.38, just above Dave Jessup and it was these two riders that won the Best Pairs. The third heat leader was club captain, Eric Monaghan.

Like Ipswich and King's Lynn, Mildenhall also suffered from injuries during 1988, and like their East Anglian neighbours they had their share of off-track wrangling. The season started well enough. Dave Jessup had retired, but in his place Mildenhall had brought back Andy Hines and signed up Michael Coles, son of their first ever captain, Bob Coles. Both of the Fen Tigers' top two, Mel Taylor and Australian Dave Jackson, were injured. In fact, injuries affected the team so much that Dave Jessup even came out of retirement for one match in the second round of the Knock-Out Cup against Wimbledon. He saw his team through to a replay, which unfortunately the team lost. It was a disappointing season for the team, who finished thirteenth in the League.

The off-track wrangling couldn't have helped when owner Terry Waters proposed increasing the rent from £22,000 a year to £30,000. The consortium wouldn't pay the increase and Waters responded by putting the land up for sale. The whole affair had a very unsettling effect for management, riders and supporters alike.

At one time during the close season, two different promoters were making their plans for running speedway at West Row. Skid Parish was having talks with Terry Waters about continuing in the National League, while Chris Shears was announcing that he was moving the Witches from Ipswich to run Mildenhall in the British League and that their first match would be against Oxford on Good Friday. At Christmas, the Mildenhall consortium put a price of £65,000 on Mildenhall speedway but said they were willing to sell the promoting rights and track fixtures and fittings for the knock down price of £30,000, though they couldn't agree with Waters just exactly who owned what at the track.

With the new year coming in, Shears announced that his starting line up for Mildenhall would include Jeremy Doncaster, Armando Castagna and Carl Blackbird. Doncaster, who was in Australia, quickly let it be known that he had no intention of going anywhere with Shears until certain parts of his 1988 contract had been honoured. This disagreement between Shears and his leading rider did not impress Waters. With only a month to go before the season started, it was announced that Skid Parish would be running things at West Row with a new partner, Tiny White. The pair paid the consortium £10,000 and that was that. The National League would continue at Mildenhall in 1989.

Their first signing was the Dane Preben Eriksen, who had started his British career at Ipswich. Other new signings were Peter Glanz, Malcolm Holloway, Spencer Timmo, Skid's son Rob and Jamie Habbin from Peterborough. These changes meant that only Dave Jackson survived from the previous Fen Tigers' outfit. Habbin was injured on the opening day and then in their second home match, Poole hammered the Fen Tigers by 66-30. Rob Parish made way for Wayne Bridgeford, Peter Glanz broke his collarbone and Holloway suffered an inexplicable loss of form and went back to parent club, Reading. Crowds began to dwindle and a couple of meetings were down to a gate of a mere 500. Then Timmo's season came to an abrupt end as he broke his thigh in a horrific pile-up. The match at home to Stoke was abandoned with Stoke 43-29 ahead and Mildenhall had reached rock bottom.

Left: *Eric Monaghan signed from Odsal in 1986 and rode for Mildenhall for three seasons.* Right: *Rob Henry steps off the Mildenhall team coach. Henry rode for the Fen Tigers from 1979 to 1985 and was their most successful rider of all time. He returned in 1994 to take up the role of machine examiner.*

At one point or another in the season, every rider in the team was injured, even the team manager, Maurice Everett, broke his leg when the pit gate at Arena Essex swung open sharply one night and caught him. Just for good measure, the machine examiner broke his wrist as well! One bit of good news came when Eriksen and Glanz managed to finish runners-up in the National League Best Pairs, but generally the season was an unmitigated disaster, with Mildenhall finishing sixteenth out of eighteen.

In spite of everything, Parish was determined to run the team in the 1990 National League, though without Maurice Everett, who was relieved of his duties. Therefore, Skid Parish spent the close season putting together a team to represent Mildenhall in 1990. When he submitted it to the powers that be, they declared it to be below the 42-point minimum – in fact it amounted to a mere 30.72 – and expelled them from the league. National League Director of Operations, Alan Hodder, maintained he had been fair to Parish, saying that when he received the proposed team he faxed Parish, telling him he had until 4.00 p.m. to come up with a stronger team. Parish said that he received the fax thirteen minutes before 4.00, which made complying with the League's wishes 'mission impossible'. However, the following day Parish signed Danish international, Bo Petersen, and appealed to the National League Management Committee for a stay of execution, but it was too late and Mildenhall were forced to sit out the 1990 campaign. Both manager and riders were very disappointed by these events. Jamie

Habbin said: 'I'm in shock. I just can't take it in. We were ready to go.' Parish was much more forthright in his views, saying, 'I'm staggered by the way this has been done. All tracks have received a warning from the BSPA that their one to sevens have to be in by March 29 or they will face a code of conduct fine. So if everyone has until then to finalise their line-up how come we are thrown out on March 23?'

Mildenhall also sat out the 1991 season, but new promoter, Dick Partridge, toiled ceaselessly to fulfill his dream of returning West Row to active participation in the speedway scene. First of all he introduced greyhound racing in the hope that revenue from this sport would subsidise the return of speedway, then he gave the whole stadium a facelift in an effort to attract back the lost supporters. Finally, having joined forces with former Norwich second-halfer, Derek Hewitt, he submitted a late application to bring league racing back to Mildenhall in 1992.

The BSPA received the application right on their deadline at the end of January, but it was a relieved BSPA who agreed to grant them a licence. They were relieved because they had got themselves into a difficult position as Swindon, who had come bottom of the First Division refused to be relegated, saying they would rather close than operate in the Second Division. Although there was automatic promotion and relegation there was also a rule which said that

Left: *Dave Jackson, pictured here in 1987, was consistently one of Mildenhall's top riders between 1983 and 1989.* Right: *Andy Hines returned to West Row from Ipswich in 1988, having been away for two seasons.*

both leagues should have an equal number of teams. With the arrival of Mildenhall, it would have meant that the Second Division had fourteen teams and the First Division had twelve so, by leaving Swindon where they were, it left thirteen in each league and got the BSPA off the hook.

A crowd of 1,500 turned up for the opening match on 22 March to see the Fen Tigers, who consisted of David Smart, Nigel Leaver, old hometown favourite Melvyn Taylor, Jamie Habbin and Gary Tagg, compete in the Autovalet Trophy. Two more riders were still needed and these came in the shape of Ian Barney and Jesper Olsen, both signed some time after the season had actually started.

A shock win at Peterborough gave Partridge hope, but he was very concerned about the size of the gates, which had dipped to below the break-even point of 900. Then other things started to go wrong: Tagg was given a three match ban for refusing to ride at Rye House, Hewitt quit the partnership and even the greyhound attendances dropped disastrously low, with only eighty people attending one meeting. By mid-June it had all become too much of a struggle and Partridge announced that Mildenhall was to pull out of the league and close. The last meeting was the Fours round held on 17 June in front of 600 people. A rescue bid was mounted by former King's Lynn rider, Graham Edmonds, but this got nowhere and on Friday 3 July Mildenhall shut its doors to senior league racing forever.

Partridge had lost a lot of money but bore no grudges. 'There simply weren't enough people coming through the turnstiles – it's a shame it didn't work,' was his final comment.

The 1994 season saw the start of a new league, the British League Division Three, which was formed basically to provide a training ground for young riders. This was the cue to bring

The 1986 Mildenhall team. From left to right, back row: Rob Parish, Robert Henry (captain), Maurice Everett (manager), Richard Green, Lee Potter, Mel Taylor. Front row: Dave Jessup, Eric Monaghan.

Mildenhall back into the sport. Derek Hewitt resumed the role of promoter, ex-captain Robert Henry became the machine examiner, while former Rayleigh star, Dingle Brown, took on the all-important role of team manager. The opening was set for early July and, in the meantime, volunteers were called in to get the stadium back into shape. Brown now had the problem of assembling a team to take on Berwick, Linlithgow, Buxton, Iwade and Stoke in the new league. Twenty-four riders turned up to a trial to select the new Fen Tigers. Amongst those to impress were former Arena Essex rider, Simon Wolstenholme, and ex-Rye House Rocket, Martin Cobbin.

Eventually, on 24 July, and after a twenty-five month lay-off, West Row once again opened its doors to speedway as the Fen Tigers took on and beat Iwade 41-37 in front of a very encouraging crowd. The official opening was carried out by former World Champion, Michael Lee.

The crowds averaged around the 700 mark, which was enough to break even. That the team finished fifth out of six teams did not matter – Mildenhall were back and here to stay this time. Derek Hewitt summed it all up at the end of the season by saying: 'We are lucky at Mildenhall … The promoters and supporters are fully behind the club and I honestly feel we can go forward … There is still a lot of work to be done, but from little acorns big oaks grow. It's been a good experience and Mildenhall have come out of it fairly well. The ambition is there…'

With the changes in the major leagues, the Third Division also changed its name to the Academy League for 1995. Simon Wolstenholme returned, but the Fen Tigers turned up a new star in Roger Horspool. Horspool was an ever-present for the Fen Tigers and top scored with an average of 8.69, followed by Garry Sweet, who improved his average to 8.28 from 6.98 the previous year. The season started well for Mildenhall with three wins from their first three matches. In the end, however, they ran out of steam and finished the league in fifth place out of seven teams, but Dingle Brown was happy with the way things were going generally: 'It is a super racetrack with good facilities and we generally attract decent crowds.' In fact he was so happy that he decided to take over as promoter from Derek Hewitt, who gave it up due to ill health.

Crowds picked up slightly at West Row in 1996 as the Fen Tigers served up a weekly diet of exciting racing in the Conference League. Roger Horspool had decided to retire and Garry Sweet was out due to a knee injury so Geoff Powell took over as top man, finishing the season with a 9.29 average. The league had now expanded to thirteen teams and Mildenhall finished up in a respectable seventh place. Dean Garrod, an ever-present and a member of the team since 1994, continued to improve, scoring 7.13 and representing the Fen Tigers in the Conference League Riders' Championship Final, where he scored 6 points. This followed a ruling by the league that Geoff Powell was ineligible to ride in the final as the Conference League was intended for youngsters to learn their trade, not for riders like him. Powell was thirty-four years old.

Dingle Brown faced a real dilemma at the start of 1997. With the introduction of the Elite League, several of the 1996 Conference League teams opted to join the new Premier League. The league was renamed yet again – this time it was the Amateur League – and became even more overtly a training league for Elite and Premier League teams, as many of these teams entered their reserve team in the league. Mildenhall had been a major player in the old Second

Roger Horspool was ever present in 1995, but then decided to retire. He returned in 1998 as team manager.

Division in the 1970s and 1980s and the supporters were used to something better than just a training league, but Brown was concerned that the gates would not sustain a Premier League outfit. Neither league really suited Mildenhall's needs and they spent 1997 trapped in something of a 'twilight zone', as the *Speedway Star* so accurately and graphically termed it. In the end, Brown opted for the Amateur League as he felt that to gamble everything on the Premier League could lead to the track's closure and once closed it would probably never open again.

Mildenhall's approach to the league was again summed up by the exclusion of Geoff Powell from the Amateur League Riders' Championship on the grounds that he was too old. Along with Dean Garrod and Garry Sweet, Powell proved to be the backbone of the team, which finished fifth in the league of thirteen. Towards the end of the season they were joined by Gavin Hedge, the son of former World Finalist, Trevor, from Ryde. Gavin finished the season with an average of 9.0, just behind Powell's 9.79.

All in all, Brown was frustrated by the set-up, not least because he was only able to run twelve home meetings during the season, and was hoping that the organisation of the League would change in 1998.

Mildenhall got their wish as the old Conference League returned in 1998, albeit with just five teams: Mildenhall, Buxton, Linlithgow, Skegness and St Austell. Roger Horspool was appointed team manager and Geoff Powell returned yet again to finish top of the averages with 8.34. Garry Sweet was also back as was team captain, Dean Garrod. Mark Thompson turned out regularly for the team, but in all Mildenhall used sixteen different riders in a campaign which only totalled twenty-five matches. The team finished third in the league and reached the final of the Knock-Out Cup, losing to St Austell in the final.

Mildenhall's luck was so bad in 1999 that Dingle Brown summed it up by saying, 'Had we been the only team in the league, we still wouldn't have won the championship'. It all started off well despite the loss of top man Geoff Powell to his home town track of Workington. Garry Sweet, Dean Garrod and Mark Thompson all stayed on. They were joined by Gavin Hedge, Phil Ambrose, Andrew Moore and later Barrie Evans. Phil Knowles was signed up to replace Powell as top man. There was a strong backstage team with Roger Horspool as team manager and Maurice Morley helping out with the track. Race night was switched to Saturday in the hope of bringing in bigger crowds.

All of Brown's hopes were frustrated as bad weather caused a number of cancellations, Ambrose quit due to continuing mechanical problems, Knowles was not the replacement Brown had hoped for, Hedge and Moore were injured and so it went on. Mildenhall finished in fifth place out of the seven teams in the Conference League, which for once kept its name. They won just four matches out of twelve. Gavin Hedge topped the averages while Steve Camden proved to be a bit of a surprise package. Signed up midway through the season and not having ridden for four years, he took the runner-up spot in the Conference League Riders' Championship final. There is no doubt, though, that the find of the season was fifteen-year-old Barrie Evans. Overlooked for selection in the Fen Tigers first match of the season, he scored 12, paid 13, on his debut and never looked back, finishing the season as number two to Hedge, with an average of 7.95. In fact his home average was better than Hedge's at 8.45.

Dingle Brown was able to finish on an optimistic note, however, when he said that 'these really are improving times for speedway and right now there has been no better time for anybody to be involved in speedway. The progress is there through the Youth Development, the Conference, the Premier and Elite Leagues. I believe that the foundations for the sport are firmly in place and that we are on an upward trend.'

Dingle Brown brought Mildenhall back to life and kept them going through the 1990s. He is seen here in action in his riding days as a leading member of the 1970s Rayleigh team.

Epilogue

As the millennium came to an end (or the popular conception of the millennium at any rate), it is fair to say that East Anglia were on top of the speedway world. In 1998, Ipswich performed the Elite League treble, Peterborough won the Premier League and Tony Rickardsson became World Champion for the second time. In 1999, Peterborough took the Elite League treble, King's Lynn finished third in the league and Rickardsson repeated his World Championship success with Gollob in second place. Jason Crump was top of the Elite League averages and was Elite League Riders' champion. The region as a whole boasts four very successful venues in Ipswich, King's Lynn, Peterborough and Mildenhall, with another just down the road at Arena Essex. As Dingle Brown said, it all augurs well for the future.

It's been a long journey since those pioneers took to the grass track at the Firs Stadium in Norwich seventy years ago, wearing their collars and ties and smoking their cigarettes. At times it has been full of excitement, at times heartbreaking, but for all fans in East Anglia let's hope for at least another seventy years of great speedway.

The thrills, excitement and heartbreaks of speedway: J. West comes to grief at the first meeting ever held at the Firs on 19 August 1930.